DREAM DELIVERANCE

DREAM DELIVERANCE

ADEOLU AKIN-ABRAHAM

Akin-Abraham Publications.
London.

Published 2014.

ISBN 978-0-9557789-8-8

Cover design by Adeolu Akin-Abraham

Printed in the UK.

All Scripture is from the King James Version.

Published by:
Akin-Abraham Publications, 5 Lanridge Road, London SE2 9SJ.

Email the author at: akinabrahams@yahoo.co.uk

CONTENTS:

INTRODUCTION

My last book on dreams, *"When you have a demonic dream,"* has been a best seller. Pastors, Deliverance Ministers and Counsellors continue to demand for the book. The first print sold out within a very short time. This latest book is a sequel to the earlier paperback. *Dream Deliverance* is even more functional, enhanced and repackaged.

The world of dreams is mysterious and compelling as it disregards the laws of reality. One of my greatest challenges as a Minister of God is the role of having to interpret various dreams and offering prayer solutions, almost on a daily basis.

I once came across, two intriguing contributions to a Christian Internet blog. The first person had a worried enquiry. This individual had a terrifying, demonic dream that she had no clue of tackling.

However, the next person had vivid dreams about demonic presence that he or she could hardly breathe. This person's only weapon was the sign of the cross and to recite Psalms 91 to ward off the wicked dream. It was an inappropriate and weak choice of warfare in the given circumstance. Hence it was a futile and ineffective response to demonic dream.

These persons were desperately hoping that someone would read their ordeals and provide solutions. There is no doubt that people have demonic dreams. It will take a lot more than just saying Psalm 91 and "The Lord's Prayer", to secure victory over demonic dreams.

The Bible says, *"But while men slept, his enemy came and sowed tares among the wheat, and went his way."* You must not allow the enemy to sow destruction into your life in the dream *and go away!* This book will not allow the enemies of your life to escape. The powerful prayers in this book will give you the appropriate response against evil dreams.

Notwithstanding, it is not all dreams that are demonic. In fact, there are delightful dreams that when we have them, we need to pray exhaustively, for their manifestations. We obviously have no problem with good dreams. It is therefore, necessary to focus on bad dreams and thrash them without delay when they occur.

Prayer books that deal with demonic dreams can never be sufficient for the use of millions of people that are hungry for remedies for demonic dreams. Unfortunately, most of the books available now on dreams, are interpretations without solutions.

You will find this book extremely useful against the powers of the night and for this reason, it must not leave your bedside when you lie down to sleep. It is the Lord's desire that when you lie down, you should not be afraid and for your dream to be sweet. (Proverbs 3:24.)

ABOUT DREAMS.

Dream is a vision or revelation which occurs in the night, when a person is deeply asleep. In the book of Job 33:15, the bible describes a dream clearly: *"In a dream, in a vision of the night, when deep sleep falleth upon men, in slumberings upon the bed;"* In other words, one cannot have a dream unless one is dead asleep. However, a vision is something that occurs when a person is awake.

God can cause a dream for a variety of reasons. However, we will look at the two common reasons as other possible reasons emerge from the two main reasons.

It can be for a warning. This is to alert or tip off concerning an imminent danger. One of such examples was when Joseph, the father of Jesus, was warned of the Lord to escape into Egypt with baby Jesus because of King Herod that was planning to eliminate the young boy.

"And when they were departed, behold, the angel of the Lord appeareth to Joseph in a dream, saying, Arise, and take the young child and his mother, and flee into Egypt, and be thou there until I bring thee word: for Herod will seek the young child to destroy him." (Matthew 2:13).

God can create a dream to provide an insight into the future. This is known as prophecy. One of the notable examples was Joseph, who was able to see through dreams, the success that awaited him in the future. His dreams came to pass when he became the Lord over his brothers.

"And Joseph was the governor over the land, and he it was that sold to all the people of the land: and Joseph's brethren came, and bowed down themselves before him with their faces to the earth." (Genesis 42:6).

Dreams are to prepare us for potential threats or fortune in the future. However, not all dreams come from God even though dreams from God are increasing today. Dreams can come from three sources:

1. **From the soul.** This is one's mind and emotions. If a person watched a horror film the night before his or her sleep or equivalently had listened to horrific stories, the dream of such a person might be unpleasant. Therefore, a troubled mind before sleep, might lead to an upset dream. This is not from God. While the body settles to rest, the mind can continue functioning and thinking about the

terrible information that it had acquired. Consider these scriptures:

"For a dream cometh through the multitude of business; and a fool's voice is known by multitude of words." Ecclesiastes 5:3.

"It shall even be as when an hungry man dreameth, and, behold, he eateth; but he awaketh, and his soul is empty: or as when a thirsty man dreameth, and, behold, he drinketh; but he awaketh, and, behold, he is faint, and his soul hath appetite: so shall the multitude of all the nations be, that fight against mount Zion." Isaiah 29:8.

2. **From God, through the Holy Spirit.** This can either be for warning or to reveal prophesy as I earlier mentioned. Dreams flourished in the Bible. God is still in the business of speaking to us. Everyone needs information from God. Everybody dreams, the problem is that the devil is making sure many people do not remember their dreams so that they will not know what to pray about. It is required of a person to pray to God for empowerment to retain his or her dreams.

3. **The third source is from demons.** This is the realm of the prayers in this book. The Bible warns that Satan can transform himself into an angel of light in 2 Corinthians 11:14. Hence, we must not be surprised that Satan sponsors demonic dreams against lives.

Demonic forces still try to attack people in their dreams. Fearful dreams are largely the rubber stamp of Satan, and it is sin that opens the doors to such evil dreams. A lot of people have had different kinds of demonic dreams and had paid seriously because of them. Facts abound about people that had suffered immensely, one way or the other, or had even died just because they suffered demonic dreams.

People can be poisoned in the dream through demonic food or receive arrows and bullets that will instantly manifest in the physical. Believers should learn to rise immediately against evil dreams with earnest prayers so that they do not materialise. The prayers in this book are strictly against demonic or witchcraft sponsored dreams. One has to determine whether a dream is from one's soul, mind or emotions as a result of one's worries or whether it is the enemy that is sponsoring evil dreams so as to eliminate one's destiny. However, when a person has a demonic dream he or she will surely know.

GETTING STARTED:

You should make this *significant routine* whenever you want to begin any of the prayer segments.

- ✓ Firstly, undergo powerfully, a session of praise and worship that will lift your heart into the happy presence and peace of God. The power of worship will provide the channel for God's power to operate in your circumstance.
- ✓ Secondly, always ask God for forgiveness of the sins in your life. The eyes of the Lord run to and fro throughout the whole earth, to show Himself strong on behalf of those whose hearts are perfect toward Him and not in the interest of a sinner. The prayers will only work for you after you have pleaded for pardon and made a u-turn from any wrongdoing.
- ✓ Thirdly, believe God and thank Him by faith for answers to your petitions.

- ✓ Fourthly, soak yourself and your environment intensely in the blood of Jesus and the fire of the Holy Ghost.

Caution:

Every chosen prayer section must be prayed with hostility that is free of sympathy towards the enemy of your destiny, for a minimum of 7 successive nights. For more effective results, the prayers can be prayed for 14 or 21 uninterrupted nights. The prayers must go well beyond the midnight on every occasion.

Prayer points that order a power, spirit or thing to pass on or go dead are directed to cause expiration of their effects on your life. There is no prayer point directed at personalities.

This book will transform your destiny forever in the name of Jesus.

1. EATING AND DRINKING.

It is regrettable that many people are being led to believe that eating food in the dream often stands for love, friendship, ambition, sex or pleasure in one's life.

When I was young, I was ignorant. Anytime I dreamt of eating in the dream, I would make sure I ate the same food when I woke up. However, my perception changed when a relation that was hale and hearty woke up from a dream and immediately started vomiting. She said she took soft drink in her sleep. She was quickly rushed to the hospital and in hours, she was dead. The evil night caterers are real. They have the agenda to steal, kill and destroy.

Many lives are being paralysed, and others wasted by demonic food and drink in the dream. If you ate or drank in your dream, you would have to evacuate the harmful deposits in your life. A man once had a living snake moving about in his body and whenever I laid my hand on him, the snake would be agitated. After serious prayers, the snake vanished. However, the man said the enemy afterwards replaced the snake with a millipede!

There are lots of demonic transfers through eating and drinking in the dream. The prayers in this segment are to remove the demonic deposits and set you free from their effects. It does not matter who you ate or drank with, you must pray vigorously to terminate any evil plan for your life.

DEEPLY CONSIDER THESE SCRIPTURES:

Mark 16:18: They shall take up serpents; and if they drink any deadly thing, it shall not hurt them; they shall lay hands on the sick, and they shall recover.

Deuteronomy 32:32-35: For their vine is of the vine of Sodom, and of the fields of Gomorrah: their grapes are grapes of gall, their clusters are bitter:
Their wine is the poison of dragons, and the cruel venom of asps.
Is not this laid up in store with me, and sealed up among my treasures?
To me belongeth vengeance and recompence; their foot shall slide in due time: for the day of their calamity is at hand, and the things that shall come upon them make haste.

Revelation 13:10: He that leadeth into captivity shall go into captivity: he that killeth with the sword must be killed with the sword. Here is the patience and the faith of the saints.

Prayers:

1. I rewind the demonic dream that I had with the hand of God, in the name of Jesus.
2. Let the presence of God manifest now and bring back for destruction, every evil power of the night assigned against me, in the name of Jesus.
3. Presence of God, swallow every presence of evil in my life in the name of Jesus.
4. It is written in the word of God and I believe it, that when I shall drink any deadly thing; it shall not hurt me in the name of Jesus.
5. Every poison of the dragon and the venom of the serpent in my vessel, come out by fire in the name of Jesus.
6. I vomit by fire, every food and drink that I had taken from the table of darkness, in the name of Jesus. (*Spend quality time on this prayer point and exercise it.)*
7. Satanic drink in my body, dry up in the name of Jesus.
8. Satanic food that had digested in my body, dry up by fire in the name of Jesus.
9. Every night caterer that served me in the dream, come back by fire and swallow your food, in the name of Jesus.

10. I overturn the table of darkness prepared against me in the name of Jesus.
11. Blood of Jesus, flush my vessel in the name of Jesus.
12. Holy Ghost fire, purge me in the name of Jesus.
13. Every expectation of my enemies over my life, waste in the name of Jesus.
14. Father Lord, hasten and destroy every power designated against my destiny in the name of Jesus.
15. Every power, delegated to lead me into captivity expire in the name of Jesus.
16. Lord Jesus, cause the foot of my enemies to slide and let the day of their calamity manifest, in the name of Jesus.
17. My vessel, reject every evil deposit assigned against you in the name of Jesus.
18. Any weakness in my body, as a result of evil consumption, receive strength in the name of Jesus.
19. I shall not eat the food of my enemies in the name of Jesus.
20. Wicked powers assigned to recreate me; you will not succeed, in the name of Jesus.
21. Every damage done to any organ of my body as a result of evil consumption be rectified in the name of Jesus.
22. Every damage done to my destiny, be reversed in the name of Jesus.

23. I set on fire, any evil kitchen constructed to feed me, in the name of Jesus.
24. Evil hands mandated to feed me, wither in the name of Jesus.
25. I recover every good thing that I have lost to satanic night caterers in the name of Jesus.
26. Angels of fire, guard my mouth gate against demonic entry in the name of Jesus.
27. I receive complete deliverance by faith, from every evil that had been done against me during the hours of the night, in the name of Jesus.
28. Every disaster programmed against me during the hours of the night of the night backfire in the name of Jesus.
29. Any agreement in the heavens to waste my life, waste in the name of Jesus.
30. I declare by faith that I am delivered by the power in the blood of Jesus.
31. I believe by faith that all the prayers that I have prayed in this segment have delivered me in the name of Jesus.
32. Thank the Lord for evacuating, every evil consumption from your vessel.

2. HAIR RELATED.

One must not joke with dreams that relate to haircut, for such dreams are usually indications of hardship, trouble and burden. If you find yourself, suddenly bald in your dream your honour and strength are under affliction.

A woman woke up one day and discovered a substantial portion of her hair had disappeared at the middle of her head. The space left on her hair was so bald, as if no hair had ever grown on it. Soon after the discovery, her marriage suffered serious attack. If you dreamt that your hair or head had been tampered with, you would need to pray earnestly against attack on your glory.

The bible says “Ephraim's glory will fly away like a bird.” If your dignity had flown away, you can pray and command it to fly back to you. This section deals with evil dreams relating to afflictions and tampering of your glory.

DEEPLY CONSIDER THESE SCRIPTURES:

Judges 16:22: Howbeit the hair of his head began to grow again after he was shaven.

Matthew 10:28-30: And fear not them which kill the body, but are not able to kill the soul: but rather fear him which is able to destroy both soul and body in hell.
Are not two sparrows sold for a farthing? and one of them shall not fall on the ground without your Father.
But the very hairs of your head are all numbered.

Daniel 3:27: And the princes, governors, and captains, and the king's counsellors, being gathered together, saw these men, upon whose bodies the fire had no power, nor was an hair of their head singed, neither were their coats changed, nor the smell of fire had passed on them.

Luke 21:17-18: And ye shall be hated of all men for my name's sake.
But there shall not an hair of your head perish.

Psalm 3:3: But thou, O LORD, art a shield for me; my glory, and the lifter up of mine head.

Revelation 13:10: He that leadeth into captivity shall go into captivity: he that killeth with the sword must be killed with the sword. Here is the patience and the faith of the saints.

Prayers:

1. I rewind in the name of Jesus every evil dream that I had, in the name of Jesus.
2. As mountains surround Jerusalem, O Lord, surround my dwelling in the name of Jesus.
3. I summon every evil power that visited me in the dream for the judgement of God, in the name of Jesus.
4. Evil unity in the heavens to waste my life, I disunite you, in the name of Jesus.
5. Fire of God, incubate my head and glory and protect me from evil traders, in the name of Jesus.
6. You mine head, reject evil manipulation in the name of Jesus.
7. I cover my head and my glory with the blood of Jesus.
8. I am not afraid of powers that can kill the body but cannot kill the soul therefore; I command every work of darkness that is against me, to waste in the name of Jesus.
9. I refuse to be what the enemies want me to be in the name of Jesus.
10. Every hair on my head is numbered and any power assigned against it will fail in the name of Jesus.
11. Every snare of the Fowler constructed against me, catch the fire of God in the name of Jesus.
12. It is written; even though all men shall hate me because of Christ yet, none of the hair of my head shall perish in the name of Jesus.

13. It is written and I believe it, that I shall not fall to the ground without the authority of God therefore, evil powers that want me to fail in life must fail in the name of Jesus.
14. Sting of death in my life, I destroy you by the fire of the Holy Ghost, in the name of Jesus.
15. My Father and my Lord, You are my shield, glory and lifter of my head, therefore evil powers that want my destiny to fail, flee in the name of Jesus.
16. Anything in me that is making me an easy target for the enemy, come out and roast in the name of Jesus.
17. Evil powers leading me into captivity, suffer defeat by the power of the Holy Ghost and expire in the name of Jesus.
18. Evil plantation in my life, my body is the temple of God therefore, I command you to depart from me and return no more in the name of Jesus.
19. Holy Ghost fire, unmask any personality masquerading against me and disgrace them, in the name of Jesus.
20. Evil barbers harassing me in the night, catch fire in the name of Jesus.
21. Hunters of good things in my life, gather together and go dead in the name of Jesus.
22. Evil hair stylists assigned to recreate me, pass away in the name of Jesus.

23. Evil hands that had stolen from me, I command you to return my virtues and wither in the name of Jesus.
24. I wash myself and my glory with the precious blood of Jesus and I command my destiny to be restored in the name of Jesus.
25. By the power in the blood of Jesus, my shaven Samson, receive your strength in the name of Jesus.
26. If my glory had flown away like a bird, I command you in the name of Jesus to fly back to me in the name of Jesus.
27. Anything in my life, advertising my glory to the enemies come out and waste in the name of Jesus.
28. I receive power to feast in the presence of my enemies in the name of Jesus.
29. Every good thing that is dead in my life, as a result of evil visitation, be revived in the name of Jesus.
30. I command the judgement of God upon my detractors in the name of Jesus.
31. Every agenda of glory traders, backfire in the name of Jesus.
32. I shall not die before my time in the name of Jesus.

3. DEATH, COFFIN AND FUNERAL.

When you see yourself dead in the dream or you are always in the company of departed relatives, you must not ignore the revelation. People who have such evil dreams are pursued by the spirit of death and hell. The book of Psalm 102:20 says, “God has the power to set free, even those that are already appointed to death.”

If you see a coffin in the dream or you find yourself attending your own funeral ceremony, it is a terrible omen. You will need to pray the prayers in this section to destroy evil plan against your life. You must be delivered from the spirit of death and hell. It is reality that in families or relationships, people sometimes die in quick successions. This is the work of the devil and his demons. Usually, people that form covenants consciously or unconsciously with dead relatives, end up dying.

To fulfil your days and your destiny, you will have to make the confessions loud clearly and pray the prayers in this section exceptionally well.

DEEPLY CONSIDER THESE SCRIPTURES:

Psalm 91:5-6: Thou shalt not be afraid for the terror by night; nor for the arrow that flieth by day; Nor for the pestilence that walketh in darkness; nor for the destruction that wasteth at noonday.

Psalm 118:17: I shall not die, but live, and declare the works of the LORD.

Isaiah 65:20: There shall be no more thence an infant of days, nor an old man that hath not filled his days: for the child shall die an hundred years old; but the sinner being an hundred years old shall be accursed.

Prayers:

1. Hand of God, rewind the bad dream that I had for cancellation in the name of Jesus.
2. I cover myself with the blood of Jesus and the fire of the Holy Ghost as I go into the prayers, in the name of Jesus.

3. I believe the Lord has blessed me with long life and it is impossible for me to die before my time in the name of Jesus.
4. It is written, no evil shall befall me at any time therefore, personalities and powers sponsoring evil dreams against me shall be wasted in the name of Jesus.
5. Every evil dream strongman, assigned against my destiny, waste in the name of Jesus.
6. Every witchcraft gathering against my life during the hours of the night, scatter and perish in the name of Jesus.
7. You the idol of my father's house that has refused to let me go, you are a fraud, waste in the name of Jesus.
8. Let the mouths of the eaters of flesh and drinkers of blood that are opened against me receive the fire of God in the name of Jesus.
9. Any power preparing coffin for my life, enter your coffin in the name of Jesus.
10. Evil programme in the heavens that is against my life, scatter in the name of Jesus.
11. Every power working to kill my dream, pack up in the name of Jesus.
12. Evil decisions taken against my life by witchcraft spirits, waste in the name of Jesus.
13. Every known and unknown covenant with the dead, break in the name of Jesus.

14. Every gate of death and hell opened against me, close in the name of Jesus.
15. Any man or woman that is prophesying against my destiny; run mad in the name of Jesus.
16. You the satanic power, summoning me into a coffin receive the judgement fire of God in the name of Jesus.
17. Any power that is announcing my obituary, expire in the name of Jesus.
18. Coven of darkness, gathering against my life, break up in the name of Jesus.
19. Raging fire of God, swallow any contrary power monitoring my life for evil, in the name of Jesus.
20. You my star, break loose from evil cage in the name of Jesus.
21. Any teamwork in the heavens to waste my life, waste in the name of Jesus.
22. Every satanic sentence that is against my destiny, be nullified in the name of Jesus.
23. You my picture in the hands of evil ministers receive the fire of deliverance and I command the evil ministers to pass on in the name of Jesus.
24. Every sting of death in my dream, clear out by the fire of the Holy Ghost, in the name of Jesus.
25. Any sin in my life, that is making me an easy target for dream killers, I destroy you in the name of Jesus.

26. Holy Ghost fire, unmask any personality, camouflaging against me and disgrace him or her, in the name of Jesus.
27. Every power and personality preparing my funeral, I terminate you in the name of Jesus.
28. You the hunter of good things in my life, waste suddenly in the name of Jesus.
29. Every good thing that is dead in my life, be restored in the name of Jesus.
30. I shall not die before my time, therefore I command dead relatives, coffins and pall bearers hunting for my life to conk out in the name of Jesus.
31. It is written, with long life will my God satisfy me and therefore, I refuse to die before my time in the name of Jesus.
32. Every conscious and unconscious covenant with any dead relative, break in the name of Jesus.
33. Arrows of death and hell in my life, backfire in the name of Jesus.
34. Every evil dream in my life, fail and every good dream; manifest in the name of Jesus.
35. I believe by faith, and I am confident that all the prayers that I have prayed in this segment will bring forth testimonies in the name of Jesus.

4. BULLETS AND ARROWS.

Perhaps there is no other dream that offers little or no argument with regards to its meaning as in when someone receives arrows and bullets in the dream. Sometimes, the victim wakes up feeling the effect physically.

A man gave me a call one morning, because his leg was badly broken. He had gone to sleep the night before with no problem at all with any part of his body. He was in excellent health. However, he said he had a strange dream that woke him up. As he stood up, he slumped and fractured his leg. The leg was in a cast for about eight weeks. The enemy had arrested him and put his destiny on a shelf.

Moreover, there have been cases of powerful Christians that received similar attacks and the arrows and bullets backfired. If you have a dream relating to receiving arrows, bullets, stones, slaps, punches or any violent attack, you must make haste to fight back. One can receive arrows and bullets of the enemies and die instantly. Also, it is possible for someone to be moving about until the enemy pulls the final trigger. You must not remain idle till the enemy finishes you up. It is biblical to return satanic arrows and bullets. He that digs a pit must fall into it.

DEEPLY CONSIDER THESE SCRIPTURES:

Ezekiel 39:3: And I will smite thy bow out of thy left hand, and will cause thine arrows to fall out of thy right hand.

Revelation 13:10: He that leadeth into captivity shall go into captivity: he that killeth with the sword must be killed with the sword. Here is the patience and the faith of the saints.

Psalm 91:5-6: Thou shalt not be afraid for the terror by night; nor for the arrow that flieth by day; Nor for the pestilence that walketh in darkness; nor for the destruction that wasteth at noonday.

Jeremiah 1:19: And they shall fight against thee; but they shall not prevail against thee; for I am with thee, saith the LORD, to deliver thee.

Prayers:

1. I reverse by fire, the evil dream that I had and command every hunter of my destiny to assemble for total destruction in the name of Jesus.

2. I have not come in vain, I will not depart in darkness and my name shall not be covered in darkness in the name of Jesus.
3. I return with speed, evil arrows fired against my destiny in the dream in the name of Jesus.
4. My body, soul and spirit ward off evil arrows, darts and bullets in the name of Jesus.
5. Every arrow of failure fired into my head, you have not found a resting place, go back to your sender in the name of Jesus.
6. Any satanic decision against my life in the heavens, break up in the name of Jesus.
7. You the vessel of my life, I rid you of evil strangers in the name of Jesus.
8. My body, soul and spirit, refuse to cooperate with the devil in the name of Jesus.
9. I waste every power that is wasting my life in the name of Jesus.
10. Any righteous decree, prospering in my life, be overruled by the blood of Jesus.
11. Any curse in my family line, attracting demonic attacks, break in the name of Jesus.
12. Any mistake that I made in the past that has opened the door for evil arrows, I overturn you by the blood of Jesus.
13. Every arrow of death, assigned against me, expire in the name of Jesus.

14. Every evil power of my father's house, targeting my life for evil, breathe your last in the name of Jesus.
15. Every evil power of my mother's house, assigned against my breakthrough, pass on in the name of Jesus.
16. O Lord, give me the wisdom to excel in the midst of Wolves in the name of Jesus.
17. Every Wolf in my destiny, expire in the name of Jesus.
18. Any power delegated to waste me; I waste in the name of Jesus.
19. Every arrow of the wicked, fired into my life in the dream, backfire in the name of Jesus.
20. Every Wolf in Sheep's clothing, in and around my life be exposed and be disgraced in the name of Jesus.
21. Every deadly plan of my enemies against me, backfire in the name of Jesus.
22. Every pit and snare prepared for me by spiritual Wolves; backfire in the name of Jesus.
23. Every bullet of the enemy in my vessel, come out and find your owner in the name of Jesus.
24. Every load of the oppressor in my life, I reject you in the name of Jesus.
25. I live my life in divine health in the name of Jesus.
26. I am the carrier of the Most High God, I refuse to carry evil load in the name of Jesus.

27. Evil arrows and bullets fired into my staff of bread fail, in the name of Jesus.
28. I claim divine protection by the blood of Jesus, from every dart of the enemy.
29. Arrows sent into my life through demonic incantations, backfire in the name of Jesus.
30. The blood of Jesus has set me free from all evil arrows and bullets in the name of Jesus.
31. Any power assigned against my breakthrough this month, break down in the name of Jesus.
32. I claim my divine breakthroughs in this prayer segment, in the name of Jesus.

5. FAECES, URINE, LITTERS AND COBWEBS.

A family of six was living a convenient life in a European country. The couple were also true Christians and generous with their money. Suddenly, they began to lose everything they had acquired. It was so difficult that they were begging to eat. The woman inevitably told me the dreams that she had been having. She remembered seeing herself in a dream scavenging on a remote rubbish dump for personal use.

Also, a Senior Pastor in a church once told me about the dreams, the Lord was showing him. He found himself surrounded with so much excrement in the church that he could hardly find a position to stand. Subsequently, the Lord also revealed to him, the atrocities and shameful activities going on in the church to his surprise.

Dreaming about defilement and cobwebs signify reproach as well as affliction. If an enemy urinates on a destiny or business, such a destiny or business will be destroyed. It is wise to return evil gestures. Your destiny must not deteriorate in the name of Jesus.

DEEPLY CONSIDER THESE SCRIPTURES:

Psalm 113:7: He raiseth up the poor out of the dust, and lifteth the needy out of the dunghill;

Isaiah 4:4: When the Lord shall have washed away the filth of the daughters of Zion, and shall have purged the blood of Jerusalem from the midst thereof by the spirit of judgment, and by the spirit of burning.

Psalm 69:7: Because for thy sake I have borne reproach; shame hath covered my face.

Psalm 69:19: Thou hast known my reproach, and my shame, and my dishonour: mine adversaries are all before thee.

Prayers:

1. I cover myself and family with the blood of Jesus as I go into this prayer segment, in the name of Jesus.
2. I rewind in the name of Jesus, every bad dream that I had in the name of Jesus.

3. I command, in the name of Jesus, every power afflicting me in the dream to assemble for destruction.
4. O You that lift up the poor out of the dust, and lift the needy out of the dunghill; lift me up from my reproach in the name of Jesus.
5. O Lord, wash away my filth and purge me with the blood of Jesus.
6. I wash shame and reproach off my face in the name of Jesus.
7. Father Lord, you know my reproach, shame, and dishonour, therefore arise and disgrace mine adversaries in the name of Jesus.
8. I receive power, over any personality that has made it his or her business to hinder me in the name of Jesus.
9. Any evil covenant in my foundation that has opened my life to attack, break in the name of Jesus.
10. Any household wickedness that refuses to let me go, release me and pass away in the name of Jesus.
11. I come out of any satanic cobwebs in the name of Jesus.
12. Any conclusion in the heavens to shame me; scatter in the name of Jesus.
13. Satanic web in my staff of bread, I challenge you with the fire of God in the name of Jesus.

14. I terminate by the blood of Jesus, witchcraft dreams that have confined my life in the name of Jesus.
15. Afflictions in my body, be swallowed by the fire of the Holy Ghost in the name of Jesus.
16. Demonic powers that have defecated on my destiny go dead in the name of Jesus.
17. I cleanse my body from spiritual cobwebs and excrement in the name of Jesus.
18. Blood of Jesus, wash my head and deliver my glory in the name of Jesus.
19. Soap of the Living God, wash my hands from poverty and failure in the name of Jesus.
20. Witchcraft powers, defiling my life conk out in the name of Jesus.
21. Persistent curses working in my life, expire in the name of Jesus.
22. Charms, hexes, jinxes and webs working against my divine destiny, pack up in the name of Jesus.
23. My vessel, reject evil litters in the name of Jesus.
24. Any power, converting my life into a dustbin, I command you to pass on in the name of Jesus.
25. Witchcraft gathering against my divine destiny, scatter by fire in the name of Jesus.
26. I fire back every arrow of reproach in the name of Jesus.
27. I fire back every arrow of affliction in the name of Jesus.

28. You the power of shame and disgrace in my life, expire in the name of Jesus.
29. I come out from the faeces and litters of the enemy and I command them to carry their load in the name of Jesus.
30. Any power that has vowed to humble and disgrace me, pass away in the name of Jesus.
31. I drop any load of shame in my destiny in the name of Jesus.
32. I believe by faith, every prayer point that I have prayed has given me abundant testimonies in the name of Jesus.

6. OLD SCHOOL, OLD HOUSE AND OLD PLACES.

To dream of olden themes like old school, old house, village and ancient places in general, do not necessarily indicate your understanding of your origin or past. You do not have to dream of your past to learn from it. Frequent dreams about old places, will eventually lead to backwardness and failure. You must pray against the powers that want to take you back to square one. Powers that are determined, to lead you back to your starting point, must be stopped. Pray the deliverance prayers in this segment thoroughly, to set yourself free.

DEEPLY CONSIDER THESE SCRIPTURES:

Jeremiah 29:8: For thus saith the LORD of hosts, the God of Israel; Let not your prophets and your diviners, that be in the midst of you, deceive you, neither hearken to your dreams which ye cause to be dreamed.

Zechariah 10:2: For the idols have spoken vanity, and the diviners have seen a lie, and have told false dreams; they comfort in vain: therefore they went their way as a flock, they were troubled, because there was no shepherd.

Numbers 23:23: Surely there is no enchantment against Jacob, neither is there any divination against Israel: according to this time it shall be said of Jacob and of Israel, What hath God wrought!

Isaiah 51:7-8: Hearken unto me, ye that know righteousness, the people in whose heart is my law; fear ye not the reproach of men, neither be ye afraid of their revilings.
For the moth shall eat them up like a garment, and the worm shall eat them like wool: but my righteousness shall be for ever, and my salvation from generation to generation.

Prayers:

1. I cancel the bad dream I had because it is not settled in heaven in the name of Jesus.
2. I forbid the expectation of the wicked from coming to pass in my life in the name of Jesus.
3. Failure, I am not your candidate; release me in the name of Jesus.

4. Anything in my foundation, that is pulling me backwards release me in the name of Jesus.
5. I fire back, every arrow of backwardness in the name of Jesus.
6. Old places affecting my present life, release me in the name of Jesus.
7. Any power summoning me for failure, I silenced you forever in the name of Jesus.
8. I refuse to fail in the name of Jesus.
9. Arrows of backwardness, fired into my life, go back to your sender in the name of Jesus.

Lay your right hand on your head as you pray the next 7 prayers:

10. Every power that has stolen from my destiny, return it and perish in the name of Jesus.
11. My glory, I command you to arise and shine in the name of Jesus.
12. Every good thing that I have lost through satanic diversion and fraud, be returned in the name of Jesus.
13. I refuse to roll over for the devil; I pursue my pursuers in the name of Jesus.
14. I recover by the fire of the Holy Ghost, my joy that is stored in the second heavens, in the name of Jesus.
15. I am created to succeed and I know I cannot fail in the name of Jesus.
16. Every arrow of bewitchment and laziness, return to your owner in the name of Jesus.

17. Diviners projecting into my dream, go dead in the name of Jesus.
18. Any power that wants to drag me back to square one, release me and go dead in the name of Jesus.
19. Power of stagnancy and failure, release me and pass away in the name of Jesus.
20. I drop the properties of spiritual Egypt in my possession, in the name of Jesus.
21. Anything in my life that is dragging me backwards, come out and pass away in the name of Jesus.
22. My past, will not rob me of my present in the name of Jesus.
23. Any long-standing problem that has refused to let me go, release me by the power of God in the name of Jesus.
24. Any mistake in my childhood that is still affecting my life, I destroy you in the name of Jesus.
25. Any long forgotten covenant with failure, break in the name of Jesus.
26. Deep-rooted affliction that is making me to fail, expire in the name of Jesus.
27. Ancient powers of my father's house, I declare my deliverance from you in the name of Jesus.
28. Olden powers of my mother's house, I declare Passover over you therefore, expire in the name of Jesus.
29. Limitation in my family line, I cut you off from my life in the name of Jesus.

30. Witchcraft dreams, targeting my advancement, fail completely in the name of Jesus.
31. I refuse to go back to spiritual Egypt in the name of Jesus.
32. I believe by faith, every prayer point that I have prayed has cancelled the demonic dream of backwardness, in the name of Jesus.

7. SEX: DEMONIC WET DREAMS.

You may have heard some people respond to dream about sex, as an indication that one's sex drive is suggesting that it has been too long since one had sex or satisfaction. However, the truth is, any form of sexual activity in the dream should be viewed with considerable caution. If you remain single when you should have long been married, and you enjoy sex in your dream, you might have a spirit spouse. I have counselled many men and women with this problem.

Also, some people suggest that to dream about sex with someone other than one's spouse, suggests dissatisfaction with the physical side of one's relationship. Then again, if your marriage is under attack and you are having wet dreams with another person other than your spouse, it is a clear indication of attacks from spirit husband or spirit wife. You will need to pray against the activities of this evil spirit in your married life. Demonic powers deposit evil in people's lives through sex in the dream. The prayers in this section will address demonic wet dreams, evil deposits and covenants that are affecting different areas of your life.

DEEPLY CONSIDER THESE SCRIPTURES:

Micah 5:12: And I will cut off witchcrafts out of thine hand; and thou shalt have no more soothsayers:

Psalm 125:1: They that trust in the LORD shall be as mount Zion, which cannot be removed, but abideth for ever

Isaiah 50:7: For the Lord GOD will help me; therefore shall I not be confounded: therefore have I set my face like a flint, and I know that I shall not be ashamed.

Numbers 23:23: Surely there is no enchantment against Jacob, neither is there any divination against Israel: according to this time it shall be said of Jacob and of Israel, What hath God wrought!

Isaiah 49:25-26: But thus saith the LORD, Even the captives of the mighty shall be taken away, and the prey of the terrible shall be delivered: for I will contend with him that contendeth with thee, and I will save thy children. And I will feed them that oppress thee with their own flesh; and they shall be drunken with their own blood, as with sweet wine: and all flesh shall know that I the LORD am thy Saviour and thy Redeemer, the mighty One of Jacob.

Prayers:

1. I summon in the name of Jesus, any power or personality that defiled me for judgement, in the name of Jesus.
2. You the spiritual husband or wife standing against my life, I paralyse you in the name of Jesus.
3. That which the Lord has not joined together in my life, let not man, spirit or power unite in the name of Jesus.
4. I command the deposit of the enemy through sex in the dream, to evacuate in the name of Jesus.
5. Holy Spirit, withdraw from my body anything that is not of God in the name of Jesus.
6. Damaging marital patterns from my parents, my marriage is not available for you, in the name of Jesus.
7. Evil intimacy in the dream, be destroyed in the name of Jesus.
8. You the spirit husband or spirit wife claiming the right to my life, I command you to waste in the name of Jesus.
9. The beauty of my marriage, manifest and let sexual perversion, disappear in the name of Jesus.

10. Any dangerous covenant that is working against my marriage break in the name of Jesus.
11. Holy Ghost fire, trouble the power afflicting the joy of my marriage, in the name of Jesus.
12. Powers assigned against my glory, Holy Ghost power trouble them in the name of Jesus.
13. Anything in my life attracting demons, come out and go dead in the name of Jesus.
14. Anything in my life, that is attractive to wasters come out and be destroyed in the name of Jesus.
15. I command my bed to become fire and consume spirit husband and spirit wife in the name of Jesus.
16. Every huntsman spirit, stalking my life for evil, fall down and pass on in the name of Jesus.
17. Witchcraft powers visiting me in the dream, fall down and pass on in the name of Jesus.
18. Afflictions in my life as a result of satanic initiations, be destroyed by fire in the name of Jesus.
19. Every enemy that I left behind, that is rising up against my marriage, be disgraced in the name of Jesus.
20. Every sex covenant affecting the joy of my marriage, break in the name of Jesus.
21. Any unfulfilled agreement hunting me, expire in the name of Jesus.

22. Blood covenant in my life that has opened the door for sexual harassment, I destroy you by the blood of Jesus.
23. Any evil in my house, as a result of demonic sex, flee by the fire of the Holy Ghost in the name of Jesus.
24. I receive the anointing to pursue and recover everything that had been stolen from my life in the dream, in the name of Jesus.
25. I evacuate from my life, the poisons of the serpent through sex in the name of Jesus.
26. Angels of fire guard my gates in my sleep and in my dream in the name of Jesus.
27. I bury by the power of God, the lust of the flesh in my life in the name of Jesus.
28. Holy Ghost fire, possess me and purge my body, soul and spirit in the name of Jesus.
29. I withdraw the peace, of every demonic sleeping partner, until I am released in the name of Jesus.
30. My life, you will not fulfil the expectations of the enemies in the name of Jesus.
31. I declare with authority, that any power or personality that will dare to defile my dream again shall be wasted, in the name of Jesus.
32. I proclaim my freedom from spirit husband and spirit wife in the name of Jesus.

8. TROUBLED VEHICLE AND DISRUPTED JOURNEY.

Usually, dreams that relate to driving a vehicle like a car, bus, lorry, train, boat, and all that, imply a venture or steering the vehicle of one's destiny. However, if the vehicle suffers a break down, stop working, crash, or goes wrong in any form, it symbolises affliction on one's destiny.

Dreaming that one is going on a journey may indicate advancement or progress. Nonetheless, if the ride suffers any disruption, it is a hint of impending setback or attack on one's progress. The prayers in this section will work against evil plans against the mechanism of your destiny and also against imminent tragedy in your life. I counsel you not to take the prayers lightly.

DEEPLY CONSIDER THESE SCRIPTURES:

Psalm 139:9-10: If I take the wings of the morning, and dwell in the uttermost parts of the sea; Even there shall thy hand lead me, and thy right hand shall hold me.

Exodus 23:20: Behold, I send an Angel before thee, to keep thee in the way, and to bring thee into the place which I have prepared.

Revelation 13:10: He that leadeth into captivity shall go into captivity: he that killeth with the sword must be killed with the sword. Here is the patience and the faith of the saints.

2 Timothy 4:18: And the Lord shall deliver me from every evil work, and will preserve me unto his heavenly kingdom: to whom be glory for ever and ever. Amen.

Prayers:

1. I rewind with the finger of God, the bad dream that I had and I cancel it in the name of Jesus.
2. I confidently declare that the evil dream is not settled in heaven; therefore I render it null and void in the name of Jesus.
3. I claim victory by faith over every demonic dream in the name of Jesus.
4. I declare by faith, that I am not alone in all my journeys because Jesus is with me.

5. Holy Spirit, service my vehicle of destiny and lead me to the very end of my journey in the name of Jesus.
6. My Father and my Creator, cause your fire to go before me and guide me in the journey of my life in the name of Jesus.
7. You the vehicle of my destiny, receive the fire of God in the name of Jesus.
8. My life, you will not be diverted in the name of Jesus.
9. Any power or personality assigned to slow me down, fail in the name of Jesus.
10. The vehicle of my destiny, receive complete deliverance in the name of Jesus.
11. I declare affliction unto the vessel that the enemy is using to harm me in the name of Jesus.
12. I return every arrow of the enemy fired into my destiny, in the name of Jesus.
13. Every power that has stolen from my destiny, return it and expire in the name of Jesus.
14. Every enemy of progress in my life, I paralyse you in the name of Jesus.
15. Holy Spirit, move me from where I am to where I am supposed to be in the name of Jesus.
16. Every good thing that I have lost through satanic attack on my progress, be returned by fire in the name of Jesus.
17. Weapons of darkness meant to cut me down, turn back and destroy your owners, in the name of Jesus

18. Let the Pillar of fire that gives me light in my journey, give darkness to my enemies in the name of Jesus.
19. Lord, restore onto me, everything I have lost to destiny hijackers in the name of Jesus.
20. Destiny hostage takers, release me and pass away in the name of Jesus.
21. Satanic traffic officer, assigned against my divine journey, be disgraced in the name of Jesus.
22. Afflictions in my fortune go dead in the name of Jesus.
23. Evil storm in my divine boat, be silenced in the name of Jesus.
24. By the fire of the Holy Ghost, my life must go as it is written by God in the name of Jesus.
25. Any power that has manipulated my destiny, tumble and go dead in the name of Jesus.
26. Every agenda of household wickedness for my destiny, waste in the name of Jesus.
27. Any power that wants to convert my destiny to rags, receive spiritual decay in the name of Jesus.
28. My vehicle of destiny shall reach its destination whether the enemy likes it or not in the name of Jesus.
29. Anything planted in my life, to waste my destiny, come out with all your roots and waste in the name of Jesus.

30. Any satanic driver in charge of the vehicle of my destiny, be overthrown by the angels of the Living God in the name of Jesus.
31. Whether my enemies like it or not, I will reach my goal in life in the name of Jesus.
32. I claim deliverance from the evil dream and I believe the intentions of my enemies have been wasted again in the name of Jesus.

9. PRESSED DOWN BY WITCHCRAFT.

If you felt being forced down or constricted in the dream and you struggled in vain to free yourself or unable to cry out for help, you were experiencing the impact of evil. The household wickedness suppresses and reduces people's strength and affirms supremacy over such lives.

Where I grew up in Africa, we ignorantly believed that such an event only occurred when there was a wall gecko clinging to the ceiling or wall around you while you slept. However, that was only a superstition. If you have a similar dream, the witchcraft powers are at work. You will need to pray the prayers in this section against the evil powers that have surrounded your destiny.

DEEPLY CONSIDER THESE SCRIPTURES:

Leviticus 20:27: A man also or woman that hath a familiar spirit, or that is a wizard, shall surely be put to death: they shall stone them with stones: their blood shall be upon them.

Deuteronomy 18:10-11: There shall not be found among you any one that maketh his son or his daughter to pass through the fire, or that useth divination, or an observer of times, or an enchanter, or a witch.
Or a charmer, or a consulter with familiar spirits, or a wizard, or a necromancer.

Isaiah 48:22: There is no peace, saith the LORD, unto the wicked.

Prayers:

1. I rewind the evil dream that I had and I summoned the witchcraft powers for the judgement of God in the name of Jesus.
2. Finger of God, rewind every witchcraft dream affecting my life and cancel them in the name of Jesus.
3. Father Lord, as I begin these prayers, I believe by faith that I receive complete release from the demonic dream in the name of Jesus.
4. My Father and my God cover me with your feathers and let me remain under your wings as I pray in the name of Jesus.

5. With confidence, I announce that I am not afraid of the terror by night or of the arrows that fly by day because the Lord protects me in the name of Jesus.
6. Fire of God, surround and protect me from witchcraft oppression in the name of Jesus.
7. I receive power to shame every wicked power of the night in the name of Jesus.
8. Witchcraft load on my destiny, be lifted in the name of Jesus.
9. Evil presence, surrounding my life and dwelling, be dispersed in the name of Jesus.
10. Father Lord, release your angels of death upon every power that is making life difficult for me at night in the name of Jesus.
11. I trample under my feet, every night lion and adder disturbing my life and I command you to pass away in the name of Jesus.
12. Evil hands pressing down my glory wither in the name of Jesus.
13. Satanic legs placed on my destiny wither in the name of Jesus.
14. Father, let you covenant of peace, sweet dreams and long life be renewed in my life in the name of Jesus.
15. Completed works of darkness formed against my peace scatter in the name of Jesus.
16. You the night, hear the word of the Living God, fight against every oppressor of my peace in the name of Jesus.

17. Every dream of failure and oppression, seize in the name of Jesus.
18. Every dream of backwardness, I cancel you in the name of Jesus.
19. Witchcraft dreams designed to afflict me, I waste you in the name of Jesus.
20. Fire of God; descend on evil ministers keeping vigils for my sake in the name of Jesus.
21. Any tares sown in the field of my life roast in the name of Jesus.
22. Evil visitations in the dream, working against my life, backfire in the name of Jesus.
23. Evil eyes that see in the dark, monitoring my life for evil go blind in the name of Jesus.
24. Evil night sacrifices suffocating me scatter in the name of Jesus.
25. Any hand of darkness overpowering me, wither by fire in the name of Jesus.
26. Satanic hands strangling my life, waste in the name of Jesus.
27. Let the strength of the strongman overpowering me, waste my in the name of Jesus.
28. Any evil gathering to waste my life, be wasted in the name of Jesus.
29. Every power, masked to steal from me, go dead in the name of Jesus.
30. Holy Ghost power, unmask and destroy the night criminals assigned to suffocate my destiny in the name of Jesus.

31. My body, become too hot for witchcraft powers to toy with in the name of Jesus.
32. From now on, I declare by faith, that I am invincible to the powers of the night and I rule over every authority of the night delegated against my destiny in the name of Jesus.

10. NAKED AND BAREFOOTED.

Nakedness is common in dreams. To dream that one is naked stands for a variety of things like exposure, weakness, unpreparedness and demotion. However, I must stress here, that the basis of this book is to battle demonic dreams. Therefore, if you are already observing winds of sorrow blowing against you and you afterwards see yourself nude or barefooted in the dream, you must not take it lightly. It is an image of adversity.

A thirty year old woman had never had a male friend all her life. It became a serious concern when she saw herself barefooted in the dream. She frantically searched everywhere for her shoes to no avail. In fact, it was suggested to her to settle for someone else's shoes, which she refused. She did not stop searching till she located her shoes in the dream. If she had not located her shoes, it would have translated into serious complications in real-life.

Your circumstance will determine the aggression with which you will pray the prayers in this section. It is not a favourable omen to be stripped or barefooted in the dream.

DEEPLY CONSIDER THESE SCRIPTURES:

Isaiah 51:7: Hearken unto me, ye that know righteousness, the people in whose heart is my law; fear ye not the reproach of men, neither be ye afraid of their revilings.

Psalm 42:10: As with a sword in my bones, mine enemies reproach me; while they say daily unto me, Where is thy God?

Psalms 57:3: He shall send from heaven, and save me from the reproach of him that would swallow me up. Selah. God shall send forth his mercy and his truth.

2 Kings 19:19: Now therefore, O LORD our God, I beseech thee, save thou us out of his hand, that all the kingdoms of the earth may know that thou art the LORD God, even thou only.

2 Chronicles 20:12: O our God, wilt thou not judge them? for we have no might against this great company that cometh against us; neither know we what to do: but our eyes are upon thee.

Psalms 17:8-9: Keep me as the apple of the eye, hide me under the shadow of thy wings, From the wicked that oppress me, from my deadly enemies, who compass me about.

Revelation 13:10: He that leadeth into captivity shall go into captivity: he that killeth with the sword must be killed with the sword. Here is the patience and the faith of the saints.

Prayers:

1. My Father, do not ignore my cry in this prayer session in the name of Jesus.
2. I wind back the evil dream that I had for cancellation in the name of Jesus.
3. I render null and void, every witchcraft dream and expectations for my life in the name of Jesus.
4. Any power that has stolen my clothes and shoes of dignity, return them and expire in the name of Jesus.
5. Any power that has vowed to expose and disgrace me, go dead in the name of Jesus.
6. Any power afflicting me through my clothing, receive the judgement of fire in the name of Jesus.
7. I return every arrow of the enemy fired into my destiny in the name of Jesus.
8. Every power that has stolen from my destiny, return it and expire in the name of Jesus.
9. I refuse to serve my enemies, in the name of Jesus.

10. You the private enemy in my life, be exposed and be disgraced in the name of Jesus.
11. Every good thing that I have lost through satanic distraction and deception, be returned by fire in the name of Jesus.
12. Weapon of darkness meant to cut me down, turn back and destroy your owners in the name of Jesus.
13. Satanic warrant officer assigned against my divine peace, be disgraced in the name of Jesus.
14. I receive power to overcome satanic violence in the name of Jesus.
15. Any power assigned to strip me of my glory, fail in the name of Jesus.
16. Wicked powers delegated to shame me, stumble and fall in the name of Jesus.
17. Father Lord, hide me in your secret place and set me up on a rock in the name of Jesus.
18. I have confidence over the attacks of the enemies of my divine breakthroughs, in the name of Jesus.
19. O Lord, do not deliver me over unto the will of mine enemies in the name of Jesus.
20. Any wickedness designed to eat me up, stumble and fall in the name of Jesus.
21. Father Lord, empower me to wait on You and strengthen my heart in the name of Jesus.
22. Wind of adversity blowing in my direction, backfire in the name of Jesus.
23. Any power demanding my nakedness and shame, go dead in the name of Jesus.

24. I fire back every arrow of wickedness fired into my destiny, in the name of Jesus.
25. Satanic rage and thoughts against my life, scatter in the name of Jesus.
26. Any power that has manipulated my destiny in the dream, somersault and pass on in the name of Jesus.
27. Any evil hand that has ever stripped me of my glory and confidence, I waste you in the name of Jesus.
28. Every agenda of household wickedness for my life, fail by fire in the name of Jesus.
29. Any power that wants to convert my destiny to rags, receive spiritual decay in the name of Jesus.
30. Anything planted in my life that is cooperating with my enemies, come out with all your roots and roast, in the name of Jesus.
31. I recover by faith, my shoes of destiny and my garments of glory in the name of Jesus.
32. I declare henceforth, that I live to fulfil my divine destiny whether my enemies like it or not in the name of Jesus.

11. SCRATCHES, PRINTS, LABELS AND MARKS OF WITCHCRAFTS.

When you wake up with marks and scratches that you cannot understand on your body, you will have to pray aggressively against evil signatures. They are marks of afflictions and evil intentions.

A woman showed to me, a deep, fresh mark upon her forehead on one Sunday morning. She had woken up that morning to feel some blood flowing from the mysterious scratch. Her fingers, as she revealed, was well cut and blunt. Also, she was the only one living in the house. The world is full of wickedness.

I had seen an old woman woken up from sleep, with white marks looking like paints all over her body. It was her husband that first noticed the evil marks and exclaimed. Witchcraft signatures appear in different forms. You will have to pray the prayers in this segment positively to destroy diabolical plans.

DEEPLY CONSIDER THESE SCRIPTURES:

Colossians 2:14-15: Blotting out the handwriting of ordinances that was against us, which was contrary to us, and took it out of the way, nailing it to his cross;
And having spoiled principalities and powers, he made a shew of them openly, triumphing over them in it.

Exodus 22:18: Thou shalt not suffer a witch to live.

Leviticus 20:27: A man also or woman that hath a familiar spirit, or that is a wizard, shall surely be put to death: they shall stone them with stones: their blood shall be upon them.

Deuteronomy 18:10-11: There shall not be found among you any one that maketh his son or his daughter to pass through the fire, or that useth divination, or an observer of times, or an enchanter, or a witch.
Or a charmer, or a consulter with familiar spirits, or a wizard, or a necromancer.

Isaiah 48:22: There is no peace, saith the LORD, unto the wicked.

Prayers:

1. I summon by fire, every witchcraft designer, artist and their instruments assigned to recreate me in the name of Jesus.
2. I set every witchcraft tool and designer on fire of the Holy Ghost in the name of Jesus.
3. Every witchcraft claw and nail marking me for evil, catch fire in the name of Jesus.
4. You the power of death and hell in my life, release me in the name of Jesus.
5. Eaters of flesh and drinkers of blood, hunting my life, eat your own flesh and drink your own blood in the name of Jesus.
6. Every coffin spirit assigned against me, go back to your owner in the name of Jesus.
7. I soak my body in the blood of Jesus and the fire of the Holy Ghost.
8. Every witchcraft design upon my body, be erased by the blood of Jesus.
9. Afflictions in my body, be swallowed by the blood of Jesus and the fire of the Holy Ghost, in the name of Jesus.
10. Evil marks that had held me captive, release me and fail in the name of Jesus.
11. Satanic designer that is re-designing my life, release me and expire in the name of Jesus.
12. Witchcraft powers in charge of my case, release me and pass on in the name of Jesus.

13. Satanic night gathering against my destiny, scatter in the name of Jesus.
14. Any power that has singled me out for affliction, expire in the name of Jesus.
15. I blot out the handwriting of ordinances that is against me, in the name of Jesus.
16. Any evil covenant in my foundation, that has handed me over to the enemies, break in the name of Jesus.
17. Any household wickedness that refuses to let me go, release me and waste in the name of Jesus.
18. Any conclusion in the heavens to harass me; scatter in the name of Jesus.
19. I cancel by the fire of God, witchcraft dreams that are hunting my life, in the name of Jesus.
20. Principalities and powers that are against me, I triumph over you in the name of Jesus.
21. Every witch that is afflicting me, the judgement of God for you is to die, therefore breathe your last in the name of Jesus.
22. Effects of witchcraft scratches, marks and labels in the dream release me in the name of Jesus.
23. Witchcraft gathering against my divine destiny, disperse by fire in the name of Jesus.
24. Any familiar spirit or wizard that is against me, receive the stones of fire and go down in the name of Jesus.

25. Charms, hexes, jinxes working against my testimonies, your time is up, go dead in the name of Jesus.
26. You the diviner and evil observer, working against my life, expire in the name of Jesus.
27. It is written, there is no peace for the wicked therefore, any wickedness against my life, backfire in the name of Jesus.
28. Blood of Jesus, destroy evil eyes monitoring my life for evil, in the name of Jesus.
29. Witchcraft claws assigned against my life catch fire in the name of Jesus.
30. Satanic signals planted in my body, stop working in the name of Jesus.
31. I believe every prayer point that I have prayed, will bring abundant testimonies in the name of Jesus.
32. Thank the Lord by faith for empowering you to destroy the enemies of your divine destiny.

12. INJECTION OR SYRINGE.

Ordinarily, injection or syringe should signify healing, treatment or restoring to health. However, there are satanic night nurses that introduce afflictions into people's lives. To dream of syringe or that you were injected for any reason should be handled with concern. If you were forcibly injected and you do not know the contents of the syringe, it calls for greater worry. After having this dream, you will need to pray out demonic deposits in your body as quickly as possible. The prayers below will tackle the situation.

DEEPLY CONSIDER THESE SCRIPTURES:

Psalm 51:7: Purge me with hyssop, and I shall be clean: wash me, and I shall be whiter than snow.

Joel 3:21: For I will cleanse their blood that I have not cleansed: for the LORD dwelleth in Zion.

Isaiah 50:7-9: For the Lord GOD will help me; therefore shall I not be confounded: therefore have I set my face like a flint, and I know that I shall not be ashamed.
He is near that justifieth me; who will contend with me? let us stand together: who is mine adversary? let him come near to me.
Behold, the Lord GOD will help me; who is he that shall condemn me? lo, they all shall wax old as a garment; the moth shall eat them up.

Revelation 13:10: He that leadeth into captivity shall go into captivity: he that killeth with the sword must be killed with the sword. Here is the patience and the faith of the saints.

Isaiah 54:15: Behold, they shall surely gather together, but not by me: whosoever shall gather together against thee shall fall for thy sake.

Prayers:

1. I reverse the demonic dream that I had with the hand of God and I sharpen my prayer arrows against my enemies in the name of Jesus.
2. I command, all satanic nurses and doctors in my dream to appear for judgement in the name of Jesus.

3. Authority of the Living God, manifest now and bring back every evil power that was involved in my dream in the name of Jesus.
4. It is written in the word of God, that no evil shall befall me at anytime in the name of Jesus.
5. Evil syringe assigned against me, roast in the name of Jesus.
6. Evil hands injecting my life catch fire in the name of Jesus.
7. Poison of the dragon and the venom of the serpent injected into my vessel, come out in the name of Jesus.
8. I evacuate any venom of darkness in my system in the name of Jesus. (*Spend enough time on this particular prayer point and exercise it.*)
9. I knock down, the satanic surgery and hospital prepared against me in the name of Jesus.
10. Blood of Jesus, wash out my vessel in the name of Jesus.
11. Holy Ghost fire, clearout strange deposits in me in the name of Jesus.
12. Any anticipation of my enemies over my life, fail in the name of Jesus.
13. Every power, delegated to lead me into imprisonment, go dead in the name of Jesus.
14. Lord Jesus, cause the foot of my enemies to slide and let the day of their calamity manifest in the name of Jesus.

15. My body, soul and spirit, reject every evil deposit assigned against you in the name of Jesus.
16. Any weaknesses in my body as a result of evil deposits, receive strength in the name of Jesus.
17. Wicked authorities assigned to recreate me, you will not succeed in the name of Jesus.
18. By the power of Him that holds the key of hell and of death, every power assigned to kill me, go dead in the name of Jesus.
19. Every damage done to any organ of my body as a result of satanic injection, be rectified in the name of Jesus.
20. Any harm done to my destiny, I reverse you in the name of Jesus.
21. Evil hands, mandated to manipulate my life, wither in the name of Jesus.
22. Angels of fire, guard my dwelling against demonic entry in the name of Jesus.
23. I receive complete deliverance by faith from every evil that had been done against me during the hours of the night in the name of Jesus.
24. Every tool of darkness prepared against me, gather together and catch fire in the name of Jesus.
25. I withdraw my name from any demonic hospital in the name of Jesus.
26. Satanic bed following me about, I set you on fire in the name of Jesus.
27. I discharge myself from any satanic surgery and hospital in the name of Jesus.

28. I return to the owner, evil deposit meant to paralyse me in the name of Jesus.
29. Every disaster programmed against me during the hours of the night, fail in the name of Jesus.
30. Any agreement in the heavenlies to waste my life, go wrong in the name of Jesus.
31. I declare by faith that I am set free by the power in the blood of Jesus.
32. Thank the Lord for evacuating evil poisons from your vessel in the name of Jesus.

13. ROBBED.

To dream that one is robbed is straightforward; it implies that your success, victory or sweat has been stolen. This dream can be a warning about the intention of the enemy or the revelation of the reality of what a person is experiencing. The dream of this nature, in all consequences, should be treated with seriousness.

The bible says we shall not build, and another inhabit and we shall not plant and another eat. You must pray against the enemies that want you to labour in vain. The powers robbing you of your sweat must be terminated. The prayers below will deal with the destiny robbers delegated against you.

DEEPLY CONSIDER THESE SCRIPTURES:

Deuteronomy 15:6: For the LORD thy God blesseth thee, as he promised thee: and thou shalt lend unto many nations, but thou shalt not borrow; and thou shalt reign over many nations, but they shall not reign over thee.

Psalm 4:8: I will both lay me down in peace, and sleep: for thou, LORD, only makest me dwell in safety.

Proverbs 3:24: When thou liest down, thou shalt not be afraid: yea, thou shalt lie down, and thy sleep shall be sweet.

Prayers:

1. Finger of God, rewind every witchcraft dream affecting my life and cancel them in the name of Jesus.
2. I rewind by faith, the evil dream that I had and I summon the thieves working against my destiny to assemble for judgement in the name of Jesus.
3. I confess by faith, that I dwell in the secret place of God and I am protected under His shadows in the name of Jesus.
4. O Lord, you are my refuge and my fortress as I confront my enemies in the name of Jesus.
5. Your feathers and wings are my protection in the name of Jesus.
6. I am not afraid of the terror by night and the arrows that fly by day because the Lord protects me in the name of Jesus.
7. Any evil that walks in darkness shall not overcome me in the name of Jesus.

8. Fire of God, prepare me to pursue and overtake the night criminals confronting me in the name of Jesus.
9. I receive power to disgrace every thief stealing from me in the name of Jesus.
10. Every witchcraft power, that is working against my destiny, fall by my side and expire in the name of Jesus.
11. Every plan of the household wickedness against my life shall not be successful in the name of Jesus.
12. Father Lord, let the angels of death be released into the camp of every night criminal working against my life in the name of Jesus.
13. It is written, I will not build and another inhabit, therefore strangers in my portion, pass on in the name of Jesus.
14. You the robbers in my destiny, hear the word of the Living God; vomit every good thing that you have swallowed from me and breathe your last breath in the name of Jesus.
15. Every dream of failure, expire in the name of Jesus.
16. Every dream of backwardness, fail in the name of Jesus.
17. Every dream designed to bring me back to square one, fail in the name of Jesus.
18. I recover my virtues from the hands of spiritual robbers in the name of Jesus.

19. Any power that has sown tares in the field of my life, somersault and pass away in the name of Jesus.
20. Evil visitations in the dream, working against my life, go wrong in the name of Jesus.
21. Evil works prepared against me, boomerang in the name of Jesus.
22. Evil eyes that see in the darkness, observing my life for evil, catch fire in the name of Jesus.
23. Satanic night collectors, amassing the honey of my life, I command the earth to open up and swallow you in the name of Jesus.
24. Every witchcraft meeting convened for my sake, scatter in the name of Jesus.
25. Any hand of darkness stealing from me, wither by fire in the name of Jesus.
26. Satanic hands that touched my destiny waste away in the name of Jesus.
27. Let the strength of the strongman appointed to waste my sweat, fail in the name of Jesus.
28. Every power, camouflaging to steal from me, expire in the name of Jesus.
29. Holy Ghost power, expose the night thieves and shame them in the name of Jesus.
30. I command the light of God, to scatter the darkness in my inheritance in the name of Jesus.
31. Every good dream that has not become visible in my life, by the power of the Holy Ghost, begin to manifest in the name of Jesus.

32. From this day forward, I am untouchable to spiritual thieves and robbers and I rule over every power of the night delegated against my destiny in the name of Jesus.

14. RAGS.

There are some strange interpretations, that dreams of wearing rags can signify cleaning up former problems. It also says, that it relates to some form of uneasiness and concern over one's self-esteem! Some even suggest that one is about to make a wise choice!

Anyone whose life is under some financial reproach and poverty will be exceedingly foolish to accept such spiritually uninformed understanding. If you find yourself wearing rags in the dream you should immediately pray against losses, poverty, victimisation, disgrace and humiliation. I will advise you to pray the prayers in this portion exhaustively.

DEEPLY CONSIDER THESE SCRIPTURES:

1 Samuel 2:7-8: The LORD maketh poor, and maketh rich: he bringeth low, and lifteth up. He raiseth up the poor out of the dust, and lifteth up the beggar from the dunghill, to set them among princes, and to make them inherit the throne of glory: for the pillars of the earth are the LORD's, and he hath set the world upon them.

Ecclesiastes 10:8-10: He that diggeth a pit shall fall into it; and whoso breaketh an hedge, a serpent shall bite him.

Isaiah 8:9-10: Associate yourselves, O ye people, and ye shall be broken in pieces; and give ear, all ye of far countries: gird yourselves, and ye shall be broken in pieces; gird yourselves, and ye shall be broken in pieces. Take counsel together, and it shall come to nought; speak the word, and it shall not stand: for God is with us.

Psalm 84:11: For the LORD God is a sun and shield: the LORD will give grace and glory: no good thing will he withhold from them that walk uprightly.

Prayers:

1. I take authority, over the evil dream that I had and I cancel it in the name of Jesus.
2. I refuse to be what the enemies want me to be in the name of Jesus.
3. My garment of destiny, receive complete deliverance in the name of Jesus.

4. Any garment of reproach prepared for me; catch fire in the name of Jesus.
5. I remove every rag of poverty from my life, in the name of Jesus.
6. I surrender completely, my finances, business, work and monetary issues to the capable hands of the Holy Spirit in the name of Jesus.
7. Father Lord, you are my source of rich living and I put my trust in you in the name of Jesus.
8. Holy Spirit, multiply my income and make me a blessing to all mankind in the name of Jesus.
9. Father Lord, fill me with prosperity ideas that will change my life completely, in the name of Jesus.
10. Powers that want me to beg for bread, be disgraced in the name of Jesus.
11. Satanic designer, creating a cloth of shame for me, stop working and breathe your last breath in the name of Jesus.
12. The heaven above my head, open in the name of Jesus.
13. Evil gateman, in charge of my open heaven, tumble and pass on in the name of Jesus.
14. Witchcraft powers, that want me to beg for bread, pass away in the name of Jesus.
15. Any power, draining the milk and honey of my life, go dead in the name of Jesus.
16. My divine helpers, wherever you are, arise and locate me now in the name of Jesus.

17. The word of God says the righteous cannot beg for bread therefore, I shall not beg for bread in the name of Jesus.
18. O earth, open up and swallow all the enemies of my prosperity in the name of Jesus.
19. Power from my father's house, sitting upon my wealth, I unseat you in the name of Jesus.
20. Evil programme in the heavens that are against my financial breakthrough, scatter by the blood of Jesus.
21. O God arise and sanction me to flourish in the name of Jesus.
22. Every garment of poverty upon my life, I rip you off in the name of Jesus.
23. O Lord, change my garment of reproach and dress me with prosperity in the name of Jesus.
24. Evil ancestral influence against my prosperity, I silence you by the blood of Jesus.
25. Every dream of poverty, release me and fail in the name of Jesus.
26. Hardship of my father's house and my mother's house, release me and pass away in the name of Jesus.
27. Every agenda of the thief for my finances shall be disgraced in the name of Jesus.
28. I command to boomerang, every witchcraft dream sponsored against my life in the name of Jesus.
29. I receive divine direction to locate the wealth of the gentiles in the name of Jesus.

30. I dip my hands into the milk and honey of this nation in the name of Jesus.
31. I refuse to be the product of any evil dream; therefore, what God has not settled in heaven shall not settle in my life in the name of Jesus.
32. Witchcraft imaginations and dreams of worn-out, tattered and torn condition against me shall not stand, for I will live to declare the goodness of God in the land of the living in the name of Jesus.

15. EVIL PRESENCE.

As soon as a person senses the encroachment of demonic powers in the sleep, one will have to pray urgent prayers to ward off evil spirit. People do get frightened out of sleep due to evil presence that they call nightmares. The objective of this evil spirit, is to haunt, steal and destroy lives. The best approach in this condition is to confront boldly, the evil powers. One must not entertain fear, for God has not given us the spirit of fear; but of power, and of love, and of a sound mind. (2 Timothy 1:17).

The prayers you are about to pray will not only protect you against these evil powers but will also destroy them. The Lord is your light and your salvation; whom shall you fear? The Lord is the strength of your life; of whom shall you be afraid? When the wicked, even your enemies and your foes, come upon you to eat up your flesh, they will stumble and fall. (Psalm 27:1-2).

DEEPLY CONSIDER THESE SCRIPTURES:

Psalm 27:1-2: The LORD is my light and my salvation; whom shall I fear? the LORD is the strength of my life; of whom shall I be afraid?

When the wicked, even mine enemies and my foes, came upon me to eat up my flesh, they stumbled and fell.

Isaiah 50:7: For the Lord GOD will help me; therefore shall I not be confounded: therefore have I set my face like a flint, and I know that I shall not be ashamed.

Acts 4:29: And now, Lord, behold their threatenings: and grant unto thy servants, that with all boldness they may speak thy word,

Psalm 2:1-4: Why do the heathen rage, and the people imagine a vain thing? The kings of the earth set themselves, and the rulers take counsel together, against the LORD, and against his anointed, saying,
Let us break their bands asunder, and cast away their cords from us.
He that sitteth in the heavens shall laugh: the LORD shall have them in derision.

Prayers:

1. I wind back the evil dream for cancellation in the name of Jesus.
2. I challenge every evil visitation and cancel their effects in my life in the name of Jesus.

3. Blood of Jesus, drench my home and chase out every appearance of evil in the name of Jesus.
4. Holy Ghost fire, saturate my entire household and purge it in the name of Jesus.
5. Every power, sponsoring evil against my life, go dead in the name of Jesus.
6. Satanic door keepers, opening the door of my life for strangers, tumble and go dead in the name of Jesus.
7. Thou power of God, surround and protect me from witchcraft cruelty in the name of Jesus.
8. Presence of the Holy Ghost, replace the presence of evil in my home in the name of Jesus.
9. Every evil spirit supervising my affairs, depart from my life in the name of Jesus.
10. I charge my life, family and home to become too hot for demons to occupy in the name of Jesus.
11. Evil presence, surrounding my life and dwelling, be dispersed in the name of Jesus.
12. O heavens that fought against Sisera, fight against the enemies of my peace in the name of Jesus.
13. O heavens, open up and swallow witchcraft strategy that is against my life in the name of Jesus.
14. Dream of failure and poverty, seize in the name of Jesus.
15. Dream of backwardness, I cancel you in the name of Jesus.

16. Witchcraft dreams designed to afflict me I cancel you in the name of Jesus.
17. Evil visitations in the dream, working against my life, boomerang in the name of Jesus.
18. My captured glory in witchcraft custody, be released in the name of Jesus.
19. Night rituals that are stealing my prosperity scatter in the name of Jesus.
20. Let the strength of the strongman of poverty and reproach in my life; dry up in the name of Jesus.
21. I put on my garment of prosperity and I reject the garment of failure in the name of Jesus.
22. I disperse evil gathering that is intended to waste my life in the name of Jesus.
23. I fire back every witchcraft arrow, fired into my destiny in the name of Jesus.
24. I wash off every evil mark, attracting evil powers into my life by the blood of Jesus.
25. Any power or personality that wants me to die uncelebrated, waste in the name of Jesus.
26. My body become too hot for witchcraft powers to play with in the name of Jesus.
27. O Lord, hide me under your feathers and protect me from all evil in the name of Jesus.
28. Any power recreating my destiny in the dream, expire in the name of Jesus.
29. I am not the image the enemies want me to be; I am the image of God in the name of Jesus.

30. My life will manifest the glory and prosperity of God in the name of Jesus.
31. Evil air, surrounding my life, be dispersed in the name of Jesus.
32. Hereafter, my life shall manifest the image and prosperity of God in the name of Jesus.

16. WEDDING AND ENGAGEMENT RELATED.

Ordinarily, to see wedding or wedding engagement in the dream should indicate progress, commitment and change in marital status. Nevertheless, this form of dream can signify disapproval. One has to pray against disappointment, sorrow and disgrace. The devil has polluted dreams with his demons known as spirit husbands and spirit wives. You have to pray against the activities of these evil spirits in your life.

A lot of people have been joined in marriage in the spirit realm and thus, they find it difficult to settle down in real life. If you had a similar dream and your married life had been under attack or you had been single for too long, you would have to pray serious prayers. It is unfavourable condition if your suitors are spirits and not human beings.

Demonic wedding has to be rendered null and void. Evil wedding gowns and certificates must be set on fire, and evil engagement ring destroyed. The Lord will enable you to achieve your destiny in the name of Jesus.

DEEPLY CONSIDER THESE SCRIPTURES:

John 14:12-16: Verily, verily, I say unto you, He that believeth on me, the works that I do shall he do also; and greater works than these shall he do; because I go unto my Father.
And whatsoever ye shall ask in my name, that will I do, that the Father may be glorified in the Son.

Isaiah 51:7-8: Hearken unto me, ye that know righteousness, the people in whose heart is my law; fear ye not the reproach of men, neither be ye afraid of their revilings.
For the moth shall eat them up like a garment, and the worm shall eat them like wool: but my righteousness shall be for ever, and my salvation from generation to generation.

Isaiah 45:2: I will go before thee, and make the crooked places straight: I will break in pieces the gates of brass, and cut in sunder the bars of iron:

Psalm 107:15-16: Oh that men would praise the LORD for his goodness, and for his wonderful works to the children of men!

For he hath broken the gates of brass, and cut the bars of iron in sunder.

Prayers:

1. I call back, every evil power present in my dream for judgement in the name of Jesus.
2. Lord, if there is anything good in the dream that I had, let it come to pass in my life speedily in the name of Jesus.
3. Every evil plan and intention to waste my life, I waste you in the name of Jesus.
4. I rewind and cancel every plan of the enemy against me in the dream in the name of Jesus.
5. I scatter by the fire of the Holy Ghost, demonic wedding in the name of Jesus.
6. I set on fire of the Holy Spirit, demonic wedding gown in the name of Jesus.
7. I set on fire of the Holy Ghost, demonic wedding ring affecting my life in the name of Jesus.
8. I set on fire of the Holy Ghost, demonic wedding certificate hindering my marriage in the name of Jesus.
9. Demonic witnesses, hindering the manifestation of my breakthrough, I paralyse you in the name of Jesus.
10. Spirit of disappointment, release me and go dead in the name of Jesus.
11. Spirit of sorrow and reproach release me and expire, in the name of Jesus.

12. I have not come in vain, I will not depart in darkness and my name shall not be covered in obscurity in the name of Jesus.
13. Every Wolf in my destiny, that had refused to let me go, expire in the name of Jesus.
14. Any power, delegated to misuse me, waste in the name of Jesus.
15. Every wicked plan of my enemies against me, backfire in the name of Jesus.
16. Every pit and snare prepared for me by spiritual acquaintance, boomerang in the name of Jesus.
17. Powers, visiting me in the dream to derail my destiny, break down in the name of Jesus.
18. Lord Jesus, make your way plain before me, so that I will not go astray in the name of Jesus.
19. My Father, my Father, if I have started off on a wrong relationship, drag me back to the right one in the name of Jesus.
20. I bind my life to divine agenda and I am not afraid of evil dreams in the name of Jesus.
21. Holy Spirit, accelerate my steps to the place of my destiny, in the name of Jesus.
22. I withdraw the peace of any man and woman appointed to bless me, until they bless me in the name of Jesus.
23. My life, you will not fulfil the expectations of the wicked in the name of Jesus.
24. I destroy any agreement in my foundation that is affecting my marriage in the name of Jesus.

25. I break free, from evil collective captivity in the name of Jesus.
26. Any power or personality, that has singled me out for failure, receive disgrace in the name of Jesus.
27. The divine commitment and change, that will move my life forward, come upon me in the name of Jesus.
28. Any spirit husband or wife, that has refused to release me, go dead in the name of Jesus.
29. I come against demonic delay of my joy and I command evil expectations to waste in the name of Jesus.
30. My divine wedding gown, appear and demonic wedding gown roast in the name of Jesus.
31. I return demonic wedding gown and evil engagement ring to the owner and I break every commitment in the name of Jesus.
32. I declare by faith, that the hand of God is upon my life and I am free from every demonic claim in the name of Jesus.

17. MASQUERADES: SATANIC DISGUISE.

When a person sees a masquerade or masquerades in the dream, it is deception and cover-up of the enemies to torment. It is convenient and well-situated for the wicked to come against someone in disguise especially when the enemies are members of one's household as the bible says. For this reason, it is suitable for your familiar enemy not to be recognised by you.

The agenda of the masquerading powers is to oppress and make lives miserable. They cause problems in different departments of lives. They are the night camouflaging force that trouble destinies. It is not uncommon to see them chasing people in the dream. At times they flog victims, symbolising affliction. It does not matter, the mode of attack as it is all geared towards affliction and termination of lives.

You must confront the masquerading powers and destroy them with powerful prayers. Any human being in satanic clothing causing problems for your life shall be exposed and disgraced in the name of Jesus. Pray the prayers below, with holy resentment.

DEEPLY CONSIDER THESE SCRIPTURES:

Isaiah 50:7: For the Lord GOD will help me; therefore shall I not be confounded: therefore have I set my face like a flint, and I know that I shall not be ashamed.

Psalm 91:5-6: Thou shalt not be afraid for the terror by night; nor for the arrow that flieth by day; Nor for the pestilence that walketh in darkness; nor for the destruction that wasteth at noonday.

Isaiah 9:4: For thou hast broken the yoke of his burden, and the staff of his shoulder, the rod of his oppressor, as in the day of Midian.

Revelation 12:11: And they overcame him by the blood of the Lamb, and by the word of their testimony; and they loved not their lives unto the death.

Prayers:

1. Hand of God, rewind the demonic dream that I had and bring back every power and personality involved for judgement in the name of Jesus.
2. I bind the spirit of fear in my life as I confront the agenda of the night masquerades in the name of Jesus.
3. I break every evil covenant that has brought fear into my life, in the name of Jesus.
4. I uncover the deception of the enemies afflicting me in the name of Jesus.
5. Every agenda of the masquerading powers to afflict me, fail in the name of Jesus.
6. Night camouflaging force that is troubling my life, expire in the name of Jesus.
7. I uncover and disgrace any personality in satanic costume, delegated against my life in the name of Jesus.
8. I will reach my goal, whether the devil likes it or not, in the name of Jesus.
9. Every environmental influence, locking up my life, break, in the name of Jesus.
10. Evil powers that are detaining my progress, tumble and pass away in the name of Jesus.
11. I shall not surrender to my enemies; my opposition shall surrender, in the name of Jesus.
12. I have not come to the world in vain; I will fulfil my divine purpose in the name of Jesus.
13. Oh Lord, open my eyes to see the snares of the enemies prepared against me, in the name of Jesus.

14. Every power harassing my life in the night, I disgrace you today, in the name of Jesus.
15. Every poison of witchcraft, come out of my destiny, in the name of Jesus.
16. Every witchcraft altar in my family, working against my destiny, pack up in the name of Jesus.
17. It is written, no evil shall befall me at anytime, therefore any power tormenting me, waste in the name of Jesus. ***(Spend some quality time on this prayer.)***
18. Every battle that is against my destiny from my foundation, scatter in the name of Jesus.
19. Every architect of suffering, difficulty, burden and hardship from my foundations, expire in the name of Jesus.
20. Every designer of misfortune, sickness and disease from my foundations pass away in the name of Jesus.
21. Every foundational strongman causing problems for my life, go dead in the name of Jesus.
22. Every familiar spirit stealing my virtue, perish in the name of Jesus.
23. Every strange power, gathered against my advancement, run out in the name of Jesus.
24. Satanic powers planning my disgrace, waste in the name of Jesus.
25. Birds of darkness holding vigil against me, crash and waste in the name of Jesus.

26. Every witchcraft agent of my father's house, disguising to afflict me, I terminate you in the name of Jesus.
27. Every witchcraft agent of my mother's house, covering up to bother me, I terminate you in the name of Jesus.
28. Any unfriendly friend in my life, be exposed in the name of Jesus.
29. Family masquerade, release me and expire in the name of Jesus.
30. I break any known or unknown covenant with masquerading spirits in the name of Jesus.
31. As mountains surround Jerusalem, Lord Jesus, surround and protect me with your fire in the name of Jesus.
32. I declare by faith, that my life is a no go area for the deception of the kingdom of darkness in the name of Jesus.

18. COVEN: IN THE MIDST OF DARKNESS.

If a person finds himself in the midst of the coven or group of witches, it can only symbolise evil judgement or satanic decision to waste one's life. It is a satanic court that condemns lives. They pass judgement and send people to spiritual prisons. This dream should not be taken lightly. The devil can transport a life in a dream into their midst to afflict or even pass a death sentence and put to death.

On one night, after a powerful deliverance service on a Sunday, the Lord revealed to me a group of witches in their coven. They were not pleased about my activities. In their midst, they had a black book that contained allegations against me. Also, it appeared that they were waiting for their leader to emerge before taking a decision or judgement against me. I straight away commanded the book to catch fire and scattered the coven. The light has no business with darkness.

One will need to pray against the witches that have assembled to destroy one's life. The prayers in this section must be prayed as long as it takes until one has the assurance and confidence that the Lord has intervened in one's circumstance.

DEEPLY CONSIDER THESE SCRIPTURES:

Jeremiah 20:11: But the LORD is with me as a mighty terrible one: therefore my persecutors shall stumble, and they shall not prevail: they shall be greatly ashamed; for they shall not prosper: their everlasting confusion shall never be forgotten.

Isaiah 50:7: For the Lord GOD will help me; therefore shall I not be confounded: therefore have I set my face like a flint, and I know that I shall not be ashamed.

Psalm 27:1-2: The LORD is my light and my salvation; whom shall I fear? the LORD is the strength of my life; of whom shall I be afraid?
When the wicked, even mine enemies and my foes, came upon me to eat up my flesh, they stumbled and fell.

Romans 8:31-34: What shall we then say to these things? If God be for us, who can be against us?

He that spared not his own Son, but delivered him up for us all, how shall he not with him also freely give us all things?
Who shall lay anything to the charge of God's elect? It is God that justifieth.
Who is he that condemneth? It is Christ that died, yea rather, that is risen again, who is even at the right hand of God, who also maketh intercession for us.

Prayers:

1. I rewind and cancel, evil dreams assigned against me in the name of Jesus.
2. Coven of darkness, deliberating against my comfort, scatter in the name of Jesus.
3. Every decision and plan of witches to waste my life, fail in the name of Jesus.
4. Any power summoning me to the coven, go dead in the name of Jesus.
5. I disperse by the power in the name of Jesus, every darkness that is covering my light.
6. Witches and Wizards calling my name on any evil altar, breathe your last in the name of Jesus.
7. Any power and transportation conveying me to the coven, break down in the name of Jesus.
8. Every agenda of the wasters for my life, waste in the name of Jesus.
9. My virtues, depart from the valley of witchcraft and locate me, in the name of Jesus.

10. Every darkness in my life that is attracting evil, scatter In the name of Jesus.
11. Every plan of sickness and untimely death against me, backfire, in the name of Jesus.
12. Every poison programmed into my body, dry up in the name of Jesus.
13. Every unrepentant enemy of my progress, pack up in the name of Jesus.
14. I pull down every stronghold of witchcraft in my family line, in the name of Jesus.
15. Every priest of darkness, working against my destiny, stop working and break down in the name of Jesus.
16. Every arrow and charm, programmed against my destiny, backfire, in the name of Jesus.
17. Every ritual power, working against my destiny, fail in the name of Jesus.
18. Oh heavens, obey my command and disgrace my oppressors, in the name of Jesus.
19. Every witchcraft embargo on my destiny, be lifted in the name of Jesus.
20. Let every root of hardship in my life, dry up in the name of Jesus.
21. Every enemy of my parents, that are working against me, go down and never rise up in the name of Jesus.
22. I fire back every witchcraft arrow, fired into my dream in the name of Jesus.

23. Any power that is forcing me to pay for what I did not buy, pass on in the name of Jesus.
24. Powers from my family line, cooperating with my detractors, expire in the name of Jesus.
25. Stubborn bewitchment in my life, fail in the name of Jesus.
26. Arrows of witchcraft, fired into my dream, bounce back, in the name of Jesus.
27. Every arrow of infirmity and untimely death, go back to your sender in the name of Jesus.
28. Coven of witchcraft, release my star in the name of Jesus.
29. Every robber of good things in my life, go dead in the name of Jesus.
30. I come out, from the coven of darkness into my divine destiny in the name of Jesus.
31. I set on fire any gathering of witches hindering my progress in the name of Jesus.
32. I separate my life from the schemes of darkness and I match in the light of God above principalities and power in the name of Jesus.

19. EVIL SUMMON.

If a person is called by name in the dream, and it is not God, then it has to be the devil. There are cases of people that answered evil calls in their dreams and their lives did not remain the same again. Some people even died right away. Immediately a person answers to a demonic call in the dream, he or she must get up and reject the call and cancel it. One can also go further to silence the evil caller forever.

The prayers in this segment have to be prayed immediately after a satanic summon. Satanic order or injunction against your life has to be resisted. Your life and expectations shall not be cut short in the name of Jesus.

DEEPLY CONSIDER THESE SCRIPTURES:

Psalm 125:1: They that trust in the LORD shall be as mount Zion, which cannot be removed, but abideth for ever.

Psalm 35:8: Let destruction come upon him at unawares; and let his net that he hath hid catch himself: into that very destruction let him fall.

Isaiah 50:7: For the Lord GOD will help me; therefore shall I not be confounded: therefore have I set my face like a flint, and I know that I shall not be ashamed.

Numbers 23:23: Surely there is no enchantment against Jacob, neither is there any divination against Israel: according to this time it shall be said of Jacob and of Israel, What hath God wrought!

Prayers:

1. I rewind and cancel every evil dream assigned against me in the name of Jesus.
2. I summoned the witches and wizards calling me for destruction to the Supreme Court of God in the name of Jesus.
3. My names, become fire in the mouth of the wicked in the name of Jesus.
4. Evil priests, calling my name on demonic altar, I waste you in the name of Jesus.
5. My ears, refuse to hear the voices of the wicked in the name of Jesus.
6. I will not answer demonic calls in the name of Jesus.

7. I reverse satanic judgement passed on my life in the name of Jesus.
8. Anything in my life, that has made me a target for the powers of darkness, come out and expire in the name of Jesus.
9. Seductive charm and influence on my destiny bounce back in the name of Jesus.
10. I recover completely, from demonic setback to my original position in the name of Jesus.
11. Demonic spirits laying siege against my life and home, be dispersed in the name of Jesus.
12. Father Lord, release your angels of death upon every power that is harassing me in the name of Jesus.
13. I crush under my feet, every night power disturbing my life in the name of Jesus.
14. I command every power that does not want me to have peace and sweet dream to tumble and expire in the name of Jesus.
15. I disunite the wicked, unified against my peace in the name of Jesus.
16. Any power demanding my head on a plate, I waste you in the name of Jesus.
17. Evil priest calling my name on a demonic mirror, go dead in the name of Jesus.
18. Demonic drum, being used against me in the hands of the wicked, turn against your owner in the name of Jesus.

19. Demonic anointed tongue chanting against me, dry up in the name of Jesus.
20. I will not obey evil call and summons in the name of Jesus.
21. Completed works of darkness formed against my peace, go wrong in the name of Jesus.
22. I arrest and destroy dreams of failure, stagnancy, reproach and backwardness, in the name of Jesus.
23. Recurring dreams of suffering, difficulty, burden, problem and hardship, I command you to seize in my life in the name of Jesus.
24. Recurring dreams of pain, trouble, misfortune, illness, sickness and disease, I command you to seize in my life in the name of Jesus.
25. I command to backfire, every witchcraft dream sponsored to afflict me in the name of Jesus.
26. Fire of God, descend upon evil ministers keeping vigils against me in the name of Jesus.
27. Night sacrifices, funded against my progress backfire in the name of Jesus.
28. O Lord, let the voice of the wicked fail and cause their plans against me to miscarry in the name of Jesus.
29. I command the strength of the strongman consuming my virtues to fail in the name of Jesus.
30. Any evil gathering against my progress, I scatter you in the name of Jesus.

31. Holy Ghost power, expose and wipe out, every evil night crier assigned to waste my destiny in the name of Jesus.
32. I declare by faith that I am unconquerable, unshakable and supreme to the powers of the night and I rule over every authority of the night assigned against me in the name of Jesus.

20. ANIMAL AND INSECT RELATED AFFLICTIONS.

There are some animals that we do not have to worry about, when we dream about them as long as they are not bothering. Animals like Dove, Eagle, Sheep, Horse, Lion and Unicorn do not ordinarily symbolise evil. However, if a person is pursed, bitten, licked or harassed by animals like Rat, Snake, Scorpion, Pig, Crab, Snail, Dog, Bull, Lizard, Pig, Tortoise and Bat, they have to be considered with utmost concern. Also insects like Spiders and Flies are equally evil.

If a person dreams about a bad animal, it represents affliction; hence one has to pray against adversity, hardship, suffering and obstacles. The Lord God has given us authority over everything that He created. Every power afflicting you through animal vessels must be terminated.

DEEPLY CONSIDER THESE SCRIPTURES:

Genesis 1:26-28: And God said, Let us make man in our image, after our likeness: and let them have dominion over the fish of the sea, and over the fowl of the air, and over the cattle, and over all the earth, and over every creeping thing that creepeth upon the earth.
So God created man in his own image, in the image of God created he him; male and female created he them.
And God blessed them, and God said unto them, Be fruitful, and multiply, and replenish the earth, and subdue it: and have dominion over the fish of the sea, and over the fowl of the air, and over every living thing that moveth upon the earth.

Genesis 9:2: And the fear of you and the dread of you shall be upon every beast of the earth, and upon every fowl of the air, upon all that moveth upon the earth, and upon all the fishes of the sea; into your hand are they delivered.

Leviticus 26:6: And I will give peace in the land, and ye shall lie down, and none shall make you afraid: and I will rid evil beasts out of the land, neither shall the sword go through your land.

Psalm 118:17: I shall not die, but live, and declare the works of the LORD.

Prayers:

1. I rewind the evil dream that I had with the finger of God and demand every perpetrator to assemble for the judgment of God.
2. I believe that I am not alone as I go into the prayers because Jesus promises to be with me, in the name of Jesus.
3. I bind and cast out, every power of discouragement, fear, terror and nightmare in the name of Jesus.
4. Every demonic dream that is not settled in heaven, will not settle in my life, in the name of Jesus.
5. Witchcraft Zoo dispatched against me, burn completely to ashes in the name of Jesus.
6. Any human being, afflicting me in an animal body, I command you to remain trapped as a beast forever in the name of Jesus.
7. I claim authority, over every animal vessel assigned against me and I command you to expire in the name of Jesus.
8. I command the spirits of the Rat, Snake and Scorpion to turn against their owners in the name of Jesus.
9. I command the spirits of the Pig, Crab, Snail, and Spider working against me to fail in the name of Jesus.
10. I command the spirits of the Flies, Dog, Bull, Lizard and Pig harassing my life to expire in the name of Jesus.

11. I command the spirits of the Tortoise and Bat that are against me to go dead in the name of Jesus.
12. Every foundational power working against my complete deliverance, expire in the name of Jesus.
13. Every power of my father's house contesting my deliverance, pass away in the name of Jesus.
14. Every power of my mother's house challenging my deliverance, pass away in the name of Jesus.
15. My body, reject the poison of the serpent in the name of Jesus.
16. Evil animals dispatched to harm me, go back and destroy your owners in the name of Jesus.
17. Every arrow of the enemy fired into my head; miscarry in the name of Jesus.
18. Oh God, be God in my situation and fight for me in the name of Jesus.
19. As Paul shook the viper into the fire, I shake into the fire of God, evil animals and insects detailed against me in the name of Jesus.
20. As the Lord God shut up the mouths of Lions released to eat up Daniel, O Lord, shut up the mouths of demonic animals dispersed against me in the name of Jesus.
21. Let the Lion of the tribe of Judah; swallow every deadly beast threatening my life in the name of Jesus.
22. I bury every enemy appointed against me and my family in the name of Jesus.

23. I cancel every satanic plan against my expectations, in the name of Jesus.
24. You the beast delegated to multiply my afflictions, go dead in the name of Jesus.
25. I trample under my feet, every serpent and scorpion that are against me in the name of Jesus.
26. Evil animal and insects, programmed into my body, come out by the power of the Holy Ghost in the name of Jesus.
27. Every physical and spiritual blockade on my way to breakthrough, break up in the name of Jesus.
28. Every spiritual barrier hanging over my head, take flight in the name of Jesus.
29. I declare boldly, that I am intact, unmoved, unaffected and safe from all the attacks of the wicked in the name of Jesus.
30. Jesus has set be free, I cannot be bound by any power and principality in the name of Jesus.
31. I claim victory in the name of Jesus, over every scheme of the terrible in the name of Jesus.
32. I thank God by faith, for granting me victory over my enemies in the name of Jesus.

21. MARINE RELATED ATTACKS.

The book of Job 26:5 warns that *"Dead things are formed from under the waters and the inhabitants thereof"*. What the scripture is saying is that evil spirits develop and materialize against people from the waters. These spirits are referred to as marine spirits. Dreams about the marine world must not be taken lightly because it is the most wicked, of all demonic kingdoms. It is a fact that about 70% of the world is covered up in water as well as a large proportion of the human body. Hence, the marine has the greatest influence or control over human beings.

Related marine dreams are regular swimming in the dream, seeing or playing with snakes. Also, living in the waters, playing or crossing of rivers in boats or ferry is an indication of marine influence. Furthermore, if you see yourself wearing in the dream, ornaments from the sea or you are always playing with fishes or seeing yourself becoming a fish is also a sign of the marine spirit. Dreams about drowning in the river, bathing, washing and drinking water, are all marine related.

Water related dreams must not be taken lightly as they are responsible for most of the evil in people's lives. These spirits cause barrenness and failure. They promote spirit husband and spirit wife against marriages and cause marriage breakups. They bring about sudden death, troublesome children, financial failure, sickness and so on.

DEEPLY CONSIDER THESE SCRIPTURES:

Psalm 66:12 : Thou hast caused men to ride over our heads; we went through fire and through water: but thou broughtest us out into a wealthy place.

Isaiah 43:2: When thou passest through the waters, I will be with thee; and through the rivers, they shall not overflow thee: when thou walkest through the fire, thou shalt not be burned; neither shall the flame kindle upon thee.

2 Samuel 22:17: He sent from above, he took me; he drew me out of many waters;

Ezekiel 29:1-3: In the tenth year, in the tenth month, in the twelfth day of the month, the word of the LORD came unto me, saying,

Son of man, set thy face against Pharaoh king of Egypt, and prophesy against him, and against all Egypt:
Speak, and say, Thus saith the Lord GOD; Behold, I am against thee, Pharaoh king of Egypt, the great dragon that lieth in the midst of his rivers, which hath said, My river is mine own, and I have made it for myself.

Isaiah 49:24-26: Shall the prey be taken from the mighty, or the lawful captive delivered?
But thus saith the LORD, Even the captives of the mighty shall be taken away, and the prey of the terrible shall be delivered: for I will contend with him that contendeth with thee, and I will save thy children.
And I will feed them that oppress thee with their own flesh; and they shall be drunken with their own blood, as with sweet wine: and all flesh shall know that I the LORD am thy Saviour and thy Redeemer, the mighty One of Jacob.

Prayers:

1. I recall my dreams for Holy Ghost deliverance in the name of Jesus.
2. I summon every wicked power that polluted my dreams for the judgement of fire of the Holy Ghost in the name of Jesus.
3. Transfer of unholy spirits from my parents into my life that is cooperating with marine spirits; come out of me in the name of Jesus.

4. Transfer of unholy spirits through sex with water agents into my life that is cooperating with marine spirits; come out of me in the name of Jesus.
5. Known or unknown initiation from any marine human agent through food, money and sex, I revoke you in the name of Jesus.
6. I renounce by the fire of the Holy Ghost, any agreement with sea monsters in the name of Jesus.
7. Anything in my possession, cooperating with evil spirits, I set you on fire in the name of Jesus.
8. I break free from family idol, dedications and covenant in the name of Jesus.
9. Fetish priest controlling my destiny, release me and expire in the name of Jesus.
10. I break free from marine based churches that have influence over my life in the name of Jesus.
11. Any power and agent, working for Satan in disguise against me, go dead in the name of Jesus.
12. Any creation from the waters, working against my happiness, expire in the name of Jesus.
13. Any body of water, assigned against my divine destiny, boil by the fire of the Holy Ghost in the name of Jesus.
14. I come against satanic manipulation of my marriage by marine kingdom in the name of Jesus.
15. Any disaster and accidents, programmed against me from the waters, backfire in the name of Jesus.

16. Powers sponsoring affliction and financial failure against me, loose your hold and go dead in the name of Jesus.
17. Satanic fish and sea serpent, delegated against me, catch fire of the Holy Ghost in the name of Jesus.
18. Deadly things formed from the waters delegated against my life, expire in the name of Jesus.
19. I scatter by the fire of God, marine throne that is ruling against my life in the name of Jesus.
20. Any living thing under the waters delegated against my goodness, breathe your last breath in the name of Jesus.
21. Any power and agent from the waters that want me to die before my time, pass on in the name of Jesus.
22. Spirit husband or spirit wife, hindering my progress, release me and go dead in the name of Jesus.
23. Let the kingdom of God, crush the kingdom of darkness standing against my destiny in the name of Jesus.
24. Marine human agents in my destiny, be exposed and be disgraced in the name of Jesus.
25. I break free, from the cage of the leviathan spirit in the name of Jesus.
26. Holy Ghost fire, purge my vessel of witchcraft contaminations in the name of Jesus.
27. Marine witchcraft harassing my destiny, release me and pass away in the name of Jesus.

28. Leviathan spirits in my household, I chase you out by fire of the Holy Ghost in the name of Jesus.
29. Marine Goliath boasting against my God, tumble and expire in the name of Jesus.
30. Raging fire of God, swallow any contrary power supervising my life in the name of Jesus.
31. You my star, break loose from evil cage and satanic sentence in the name of Jesus.
32. I declare by faith, that I am set free in the name of Jesus.

22. MOUNTAIN AND OBSTACLES RELATED.

To interpret dreams about mountain will depend on how one relates to the object in the dream. Mountains are obstacles that are meant to be conquered. It is a pleasant dream if a person sees himself on the top of the mountain. It signifies that one is on top of situations. It also indicates that the individual has reached loftiness and a level of awareness spiritually or physically. Therefore, to dream of being at the top of a mountain may indicate rising above spiritual or physical mediocrity. It is a level of promotion and elevation.

However, to dream of struggling to climb a mountain or to fall off a mountain, has a disastrous implication. The consequence of the inability to overcome the mountain implies failure, demotion and trial. If you see yourself climbing a slippery or treacherous mountain unsuccessfully, you will need to pray against failure, hardship and obstacles. If a mountain is standing between you and your success, you will need to pray for the obstacle to scatter.

DEEPLY CONSIDER THESE SCRIPTURES:

Matthew 19:26: But Jesus beheld them, and said unto them, With men this is impossible; but with God all things are possible.

Zechariah 4:7: Who art thou, O great mountain? before Zerubbabel thou shalt become a plain: and he shall bring forth the headstone thereof with shoutings, crying, Grace, grace unto it.

Jeremiah 1:19: And they shall fight against thee; but they shall not prevail against thee; for I am with thee, saith the LORD, to deliver thee.

Revelation 13:10: He that leadeth into captivity shall go into captivity: he that killeth with the sword must be killed with the sword. Here is the patience and the faith of the saints.

Psalm 34:21: Evil shall slay the wicked: and they that hate the righteous shall be desolate.

Prayers:

1. Hand of God, rewind my dream for cancellation in the name of Jesus.
2. Evil dream that is not settled in heaven, you will not settle in my life in the name of Jesus.
3. You the mountain of sin in my life, delaying my divine destiny, scatter in the name of Jesus.
4. You the evil power, following my life like a shadow, I command you to expire in the name of Jesus.
5. I am a mountain mover, every problem mountain standing before my Zerubbabel, I move you in the name of Jesus.
6. All the difficulties that have piled up before me like a great mountain; dissolve in the name of Jesus.
7. Mountain of failure, demotion and trial, crumble in the name of Jesus.
8. I command the hardship in my foundation to receive the fire of the Holy Ghost in the name of Jesus.
9. Mountain of poverty and reproach, scatter in the name of Jesus.
10. You the mountain of impossibility in my life, become a plain in the name of Jesus.
11. Lord Jesus, speak by thunder and fire and cause the mountain of failure in my life to melt in the name of Jesus.

12. All creation in the heavens, in the earth, underneath the earth, in the waters and in the air, arise and promote my destiny in the name of Jesus.
13. O Lord, let the days of my enemies be few and let them be replaced in the name of Jesus.
14. Any power rejoicing at my misfortune, stumble and expire in the name of Jesus.
15. I waste every power wasting my sweat in the name of Jesus.
16. Anointing of wasted efforts, expire in the name of Jesus.
17. Lord Jesus, let a cry of sorrow be heard from the camp of the enemies of my progress in the name of Jesus.
18. O Lord, let the deadly plans of my enemies against me, backfire in the name of Jesus.
19. I refuse to fall from my mountain of decision in the name of Jesus.
20. I receive power to climb to the top of my career and finances in the name of Jesus.
21. Any power assigned against me to waste my efforts, I command you to expire in the name of Jesus.
22. I receive the power, vision and the mind to excel in all that I do in the name of Jesus.
23. O God, arise and let my enemies be scattered, in the name of Jesus.
24. Every evil that I have brought into my life by my own hands expire in the name of Jesus.

25. I offload, evil load that is upon my destiny that is slowing me down in the name of Jesus.
26. Every evil that I have brought into my life by my own hands, pass away in the name of Jesus.
27. I refuse to climb unsuccessful any mountain confronting my life in the name of Jesus.
28. Every insurmountable problem, receive solution in the name of Jesus.
29. You the witchcraft mountain standing between me and my success, scatter in the name of Jesus.
30. I advance to the level of physical and spiritual awareness in all the departments of my life in the name of Jesus.
31. The obstacles confronting my life now shall become my mountain of promotion and elevation in the name of Jesus.
32. I see myself on the top of my mountain and on top of every situation in my life in the name of Jesus.

23. PURSUED BY VIOLENT ENEMIES.

To be pursued in a dream is an unpleasant and hostile circumstance. The best position to be in the dream is to be the hunter and not the hunted. Therefore, for someone to be chased or hunted by a murderous enemy, suggests that one has angered them. The reason for provocation can be either physical because of one's achievement in life or spiritual because of one's prayers. The agenda of the pursuers is to waste lives.

However, you must not surrender your comfortable position to the enemy or to stop your prayers because of the threats of the wicked. It is time for you to intensify your request to God. The enemies that are running after your life must be destroyed. You must turn back and wipe them out. The hunters of your destiny must be tracked down and eliminated. The Lord told David to pursue, overtake and recover. The position of every Believer in the scripture is to be the pursuer. David did not turn back until he recovered all, so you must not.

DEEPLY CONSIDER THESE SCRIPTURES:

Isaiah 8:9-10: Associate yourselves, O ye people, and ye shall be broken in pieces; and give ear, all ye of far countries: gird yourselves, and ye shall be broken in pieces; gird yourselves, and ye shall be broken in pieces.
Take counsel together, and it shall come to nought; speak the word, and it shall not stand: for God is with us.

Psalm 118:11: They compassed me about; yea, they compassed me about: but in the name of the LORD I will destroy them.

Psalm 68:1-2: Let God arise, let his enemies be scattered: let them also that hate him flee before him.
As smoke is driven away, so drive them away: as wax melteth before the fire, so let the wicked perish at the presence of God.

Jeremiah 1:8, 19: Be not afraid of their faces: for I am with thee to deliver thee, saith the LORD.
And they shall fight against thee; but they shall not prevail against thee; for I am with thee, saith the LORD, to deliver thee.

Prayers:

1. I cover myself and my family with the blood of Jesus as I turn against my enemies in the name of Jesus.
2. Hand of God, rewind my dream for remedy in the name of Jesus.
3. Every right that I have given to the devil to afflict me, be destroyed by the blood of Jesus.
4. Any creation working against my success, fail in the name of Jesus.
5. I refuse to be hunted; I receive power to pursue my pursuers in the name of Jesus.
6. O Lord, let the ways of my pursuers be dark and slippery in the name of Jesus.
7. Powers that are tracking me for evil, expire now in the name of Jesus.
8. Powers of my father's house, stalking my destiny, pass on in the name of Jesus.
9. Powers of my mother's house, trailing me like a shadow, pass away in the name of Jesus.
10. Any power assigned to drag me back to square one, waste in the name of Jesus.
11. I come against personalities that have made it their business to hinder me and I command them to be disgraced in the name of Jesus.
12. I bind my life to my divine helpers in the name of Jesus.
13. I bind my destiny to every good thing that is meant to happen to me this year in the name of Jesus.

14. Every messenger of Satan assigned against me, go dead in the name of Jesus.
15. Any ungodly soul- tie with the living or the dead in my life, break in the name of Jesus.
16. Every satanic gang up to disgrace me, scatter in the name of Jesus.
17. I destroy every power or covenant that has made me a target for the enemies, in the name of Jesus.
18. I renounce, break and free myself from all demonic subjection or control in the name of Jesus.
19. I cast into the fire of judgment, any viper fastened to my destiny in the name of Jesus.
20. You the monster in my place of comfort, expire in the name of Jesus.
21. By the fire of the Holy Ghost, I will laugh last over all my detractors in the name of Jesus.
22. Powers and personalities harassing me, receive double disgrace in the name of Jesus.
23. Any sin in my life, that is hunting me, I destroy you with the blood of Jesus.
24. I bring the blood of Jesus between me and any human being that has refused to forgive me in the name of Jesus.
25. Holy Ghost fire, trouble the power afflicting my joy in the name of Jesus.
26. Anything in my life attracting evil spirits, come out and go dead in the name of Jesus.
27. I command my bed to become fire and consume every pursuer, in the name of Jesus.

28. Every huntsman spirit, stalking my life for evil, fall down and pass on in the name of Jesus.
29. Witchcraft powers visiting me in the dream, fall down and pass on in the name of Jesus.
30. Every enemy that I left behind that is rising up against me, expire in the name of Jesus.
31. Every covenant that is hunting my life, break in the name of Jesus.
32. Any unfulfilled agreement hunting me, expire in the name of Jesus.
33. I receive the mandate and the anointing, to pursue and recover, everything that had been stolen from my life in the dream and in the physical in the name of Jesus.
34. I am the hunter; I refuse to be hunted from now henceforth in the name of Jesus.

19. I will not start all over again; any power that wants me to go back to square one, pass away in the name of Jesus.
20. I refuse to be less than what the heaven expects of me in the name of a Jesus.
21. Any personality that is prophesying against my destiny; run mad in the name of Jesus.
22. You the satanic power, summoning me for destruction, receive the judgement of the fire of God in the name of Jesus.
23. Any power that is declaring my obituary, expire in the name of Jesus.
24. Witchcraft powers, gathering against my life, break up and expire in the name of Jesus.
25. I cancel any demonic dream that is targeting my star, in the name of Jesus.
26. I cancel and disband any solidarity in the heavens assigned to waste my life in the name of Jesus.
27. I cancel every satanic sentence that is against my destiny and I declare you null and void in the name of Jesus.
28. Every venom of death in my dream, clear out by the fire of the Holy Ghost in the name of Jesus.
29. Holy Ghost fire, unmask any personality disguising to destroy me in the dream in the name of Jesus.
30. You the predator of good things in my life, go dead in the name of Jesus.

31. I cancel and render null and void, every demonic dream targeting my finances in the name of Jesus.
32. I cancel and render null and void, every satanic dream targeting my health in the name of Jesus.
33. I cancel and render null and void, every evil dream targeting my health in the name of Jesus.
34. I cancel and render null and void, every witchcraft dream targeting my success in the name of Jesus.
35. I cancel and render null and void, every wicked dream assigned to waste me in the name of Jesus.
36. I cancel and render null and void, every bad dream targeting my finances in the name of Jesus.
37. I cancel and render null and void, every unpleasant dream harassing me in the name of Jesus.
38. I recover from any failure that I suffered in the dream in the name of Jesus.
39. Death, Coffin and Funeral arrangements for me in the dream, backfire in the name of Jesus.
40. Invisible satanic bullets and arrows, assigned against me, miscarry in the name of Jesus.
41. I reject reproach and I command you to expire in my life, the name of Jesus.
42. Witchcraft dream, delegated to make me a failure, fail in the name of Jesus.
43. My vehicle of deliverance, be fuelled by the fire of the Holy Ghost in the name of Jesus.
44. I turn the table against witchcraft dreams that are suffocating and overpowering me and I command them to waste in the name of Jesus.

45. I wash off the label of witchcraft from my life in the name of Jesus.
46. I decree the death sentence of every power stalking me in the dream in the name of Jesus.
47. I announce the end of satanic persecution in my dream to stop in the name of Jesus.
48. I order that my dream is henceforth, a no go area for witchcraft manipulations in the name of Jesus.
49. I command my divine dreams to come to pass and demonic dreams to waste in the name of Jesus.
50. It is written, "Forever O Lord, thy word is settled in heaven"; therefore any dream that is not settled in heaven will not settle in my life in the name of Jesus.

25. POWER TO RECALL YOUR DREAMS.

I have come across studies of how people can, with deliberate effort, remember more of their dreams and recall them in greater detail. This of course is a scientific or physical approach to remembering your dream. Certainly, there are abounding theories as to why we dream, how we dream, and what meaning we can give to our dreams. Many people believe that dreams can provide insights into our lives and feelings; that I agree with, but the trouble is, they are extremely difficult to recall.

Some of their formulas suggest that you do a number of things that will enhance remembering your dream before you go to bed.

Here are a few of these guidelines, even though I do not completely agree with them; they might be worth taking a cursory look at:

- **Prepare to get a good night's sleep.**
  It is believed the longer the length of sleep the greater the chances of remembering your dream.
- **Put a pad and a writing material within easy reach of your bed.**
  This is for jotting down your dreams each time you wake up at night.
- **Keep your alarm near to your bed.**
  It is believed that getting out of bed to turn it off will reduce the chances of remembering what you dreaming about.
- **Don't eat, drink alcohol or take medication right before bed.**
  It is said that the chemicals in these items can affect your brain's ability to remember dreams.
- **Calm your mind and body before bedtime.**
  Having a lot of stressful thoughts in your head can make it more difficult to remember your dreams, which requires profound focus.
- **Make a conscious decision to remember your dreams.**
  You have got a better chance of remembering your dreams if you really want to remember them. Tell yourself that you are going to remember your dreams (I like that) and thoroughly follow the steps to make your desire to remember your dreams come true.
- **Think about a major problem or emotional concern right before you fall asleep.**

> Think deeply about the situation without pressing for solutions or coming to conclusions. Just thinking about the problem opens the door, in a sense, to more clearly remembered dreams, and the dreams may even offer more insights regarding the problem at hand. Well, I am not sure about that.

However, dream is spiritual and not physical. It should not be handled with physical solution. If a dream is a means through which God communicates with His children then it is expected that Satan will always try his best to corrupt, block or erase it. If God is to alert or tip you off concerning an imminent danger why will the devil allow it? If God, through a dream can provide you an insight into your future why will Satan permit it? We are also aware that not all dreams come from God so there is so much going on spiritually in your sleep.

With consistent prayers, you can begin to recall your dreams by arresting the powers of mind blindness and memory blackouts.

DEEPLY CONSIDER THESE SCRIPTURES:

John 10:27

My sheep hear my voice, and I know them, and they follow me:

Isaiah 30:21

And thine ears shall hear a word behind thee, saying, This is the way, walk ye in it, when ye turn to the right hand, and when ye turn to the left.

Job 33:14-15.

For God speaketh once, yea twice, yet man perceiveth it not.

In a dream, in a vision of the night, when deep sleep falleth upon men, in slumberings upon the bed;"

Romans 8:14

For as many as are led by the Spirit of God, they are the sons of God.

Isaiah 29:8

It shall even be as when an hungry man dreameth, and, behold, he eateth; but he awaketh, and his soul is empty: or as when a thirsty man dreameth, and, behold, he drinketh; but he awaketh, and, behold, he is faint, and his soul hath appetite: so shall the multitude of all the nations be, that fight against mount Zion.

Prayers:

1. Let the power to perceive and remember the voice of God come upon me in the name of Jesus.
2. Power to hear twice when God speaks once come upon me in the name of Jesus.
3. My spiritual pipe, receive fire of the Holy Ghost in the name of Jesus.
4. Fire of God, clear the channel between my spiritual world and my physical world in the name of Jesus.

5. Blood of Jesus empower me to remember in detail all communications in my dream in the name of Jesus.
6. Spiritual blindness, I challenge you by fire and command you to expire in the name of Jesus.
7. Every unseen activities robbing me in the dream I arrest you in the name of Jesus.
8. Power of evil manipulation in my dream break down in the name of Jesus.
9. It is written, "For as many as are led by the Spirit of God, they are the sons of God." O Lord I am your child lead me in the name of Jesus.
10. I am the Lord's sheep, I hear His voice, and He knows me and I follow Him.
11. Lord Jesus, speak to my spirit man in the name of Jesus.
12. Every evil altar cancelling my dreams, scatter in the name of Jesus.
13. Satanic erasers, robbing out my dreams before I wake up catch fire in the name of Jesus.
14. Thou power of God bring to my remembrance every dream that I need to recollect in the name of Jesus.
15. Every evil garment covering my spiritual eyes be roasted by fire in the name of Jesus.
16. My ears shall hear a word behind me, saying, this is the way, walk in it, in the name of Jesus.
17. Every evil blockage of my spiritual ears, scatter by fire in the name of Jesus.

18. Thou power of absent mindedness and memory blackouts scatter in the name of Jesus.
19. Any evil visitation in my dream, be arrested in the name of Jesus.
20. My dream life, receive fire, become fire and vomit fire in the name of Jesus.
21. Thou power night pollution my life, be arrested in the name of Jesus.
22. Let my dream world become too hot for dream manipulators in the name of Jesus.
23. My spirit man, be sharpened by the fire of the Holy Ghost in the name of Jesus.
24. From now henceforth, I receive power by the blood of Jesus to remember my dreams in the name of Jesus.

26. DREAM CODES.

NUMBER CODES

1. Godhead, agreement, beginning, harmony foundation, genesis, starting place
2. Split, rift, disagreement, testifier
3. God in three forms - Trinity, wholeness, restoration, renewal, resurrection, life – existence.
4. Man, creation, formation.
5. Grace, favour, mercy, sacrifice, affection.
6. Devil or Satan, flaw, weak point, beast, man.
7. Spiritual perfection, completion, rest, newness, resurrection, life.
8. Rebirth, new beginning, fresh start, new experiences
9. Spiritual gifts, fruit of the Spirit, spiritual richness.
10. Administration, authority, divine order, law, government.
11. Judgment, vengeance, recompense, rewards.
12. Heavenly authority, apostolic fullness, governmental perfection.
13. Revolt, rebellion, sin, going back to old ways, apostasy.
14. Salvation, liberation, freedom, deliverance.
15. Respite, rest
16. Love, affection.

17. Triumph, Conquest, Victory, justifiable, righteousness
18. Oppression, Bondage
19. Faith, dedication
20. Redemption, salvation
21. Sinfulness.
22. Light, sign, manifestation
23. Death, casualty.
24. Priesthood
25. Exoneration, forgiveness of sins
26. Gospel numeral.
27. Prophecy numeral.
28. Eternal life.
29. Exit, departure.
30. Blood, preparation and ministry numeral.
33. Process of change or transition.
39. Sickness, illness and disease.
40. Ordeal, trial.
50. Salvation, celebration, jubilee, liberty, Pentecost.
66. Idol worship.
600. Warfare, conflict.
666. Mark of the beast, anti-Christ.
1000. Glory of God, divine completeness, millennium.

COLOUR CODES.

White — spotlessness, honour, purity, light, righteousness.
Black — sin, death, secrecy, shortage.

Blue — heaven, Holy Spirit.
Amber — glory of God.
Orange — threatening danger; energy to shine, force, energy.
Crimson — blood, atonement, sacrifice.
Purple — royal.
Magenta — sovereigns, royalty.
Red — conflict, bloodshed, killings or injuries, war.
Green — life, intercession, jealousy.
Gray — dishonesty, vagueness, lifeless, in despair.
Lavender — disappointment, transitory unhappiness.
Pink — achievement, victory, success.
Yellow — hindrance, delay, setbacks, struggle.
Brown — unresponsive situation, dead issues, penitence.

Some Powerful Messages by the Author.

1. Mountain Gazers, Mountain Movers.
2. The 1st Spiritual Law.
3. Shake, Awake and Shake.
4. 18 Victory Forces.
5. The two great Forces.
6. Your Gate of Miracle.
7. Fools in a snare.
8. The Mark of Sibboleth.
9. Evil in the House.
10. Fear Factor.
11. Dagger Vengeance.
12. Violence for Violence.
13. The enemy behind.
14. Believed Grasshoppers.
15. Down but not out.
16. Is it not in thy book?
17. I claim the impossible.
18. Making Jesus Vomit.
19. The anointing of Uzziah.
20. I refuse to give up.
21. Let God be God.
22. Look or Die.
23. Overcoming your Esau.
24. Overturn the Usual.
25. I come out!
26. Pay your due, claim your due.
27. My God get up!
28. Spoiling the treasures of darkness.
29. Step out of Shittim
30. Power over evil completion.
31. Power to feast before the enemies.

32. Power to fight from above.
33. Summon your power O God.
34. The battles you must win.
35. The hours of darkness.
36. The Lord's Job Advert.
37. The nature of the enemy.
38. The necessary concern.
39. The rod of the wicked.
40. Turning Northward.
41. Unlocking your destiny.
42. Victory against all odds.
43. The scale of balances.
44. When God gives up.
45. Overturning righteous verdicts.
46. Who are you?
47. The burden of inheritance.
48. Who is he that will harm you?
49. How can you sleep?
50. Knowing your stubborn enemies.
51. Revive us again.
52. The mystery of water.
53. The power of seven.
54. When they hear of your anointing.
55. As the Lord God of Israel Liveth.
56. Deliverance from stagnancy.
57. Living Above thy fellows.
58. Violent prayers against the wicked

OTHER BOOKS BY ADEOLU AKIN-ABRAHAM

"The Mark of Sibboleth" is a book equipped to overcome failure, satanic agenda and witchcraft manipulations.

"Defeating Destiny Pickpockets," is specifically written with the inspiration of the Holy Spirit to destroy the subtle, yet deadly robber spirit that is referred to as the Destiny Pickpockets.

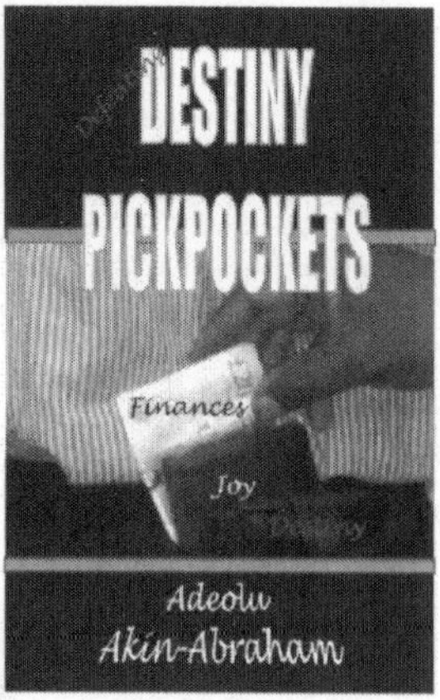

"The 112 Prayers that a youngster must pray," is a daily prayer manual for an immediate, complete deliverance as well as investment for the future of children.

OTHER BOOKS BY ADEOLU AKIN-ABRAHAM... CONTINUED

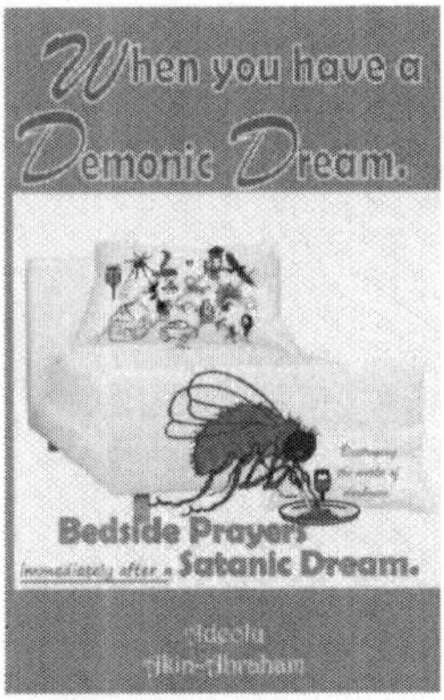

"When you have a demonic dream," is a best seller. The book is a cure for evil dreams as well as destroying the witchcraft powers behind the dream. Hence, it is a practical, bedside prayer book to use, immediately after a terrible dream.

"Passover Midnight Deliverance Prayers" could be the last resort in any deliverance. The Passover event is without a doubt the greatest freedom story in history. In just one midnight, God transformed the lot of the scattered enslaved tribes of Israel in Egypt to a nation on the road to great deliverance.

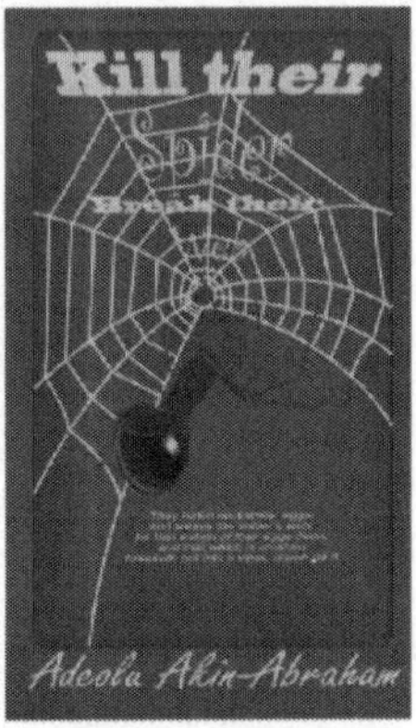

"Kill their spider break their web", is a practical and no-nonsense message against the invisible power of satanic cobweb and its evil spinner.

OTHER BOOKS BY ADEOLU AKIN-ABRAHAM... CONTINUED

"42 Days of Violent Decrees."
Set out 42 days of successive violent prophetic morning decrees and you will win the battle confronting you in the name of Jesus.